At Issue

| Year-Round Schools

Other Books in the At Issue Series:

At Issue

Year-Round Schools

Adriane Ruggiero, Book Editor

GREENHAVEN PRESS

An imprint of Thomson Gale, a part of The Thomson Corporation

THOMSON

™

GALE

Detroit • New York • San Francisco • New Haven, Conn. • Waterville, Maine • London

THOMSON
——✷——™
GALE

Christine Nasso, *Publisher*
Elizabeth Des Chenes, *Managing Editor*

© 2008 The Gale Group.

For more information, contact:
Greenhaven Press
27500 Drake Rd.
Farmington Hills, MI 48331-3535
Or you can visit our Internet site at http://www.gale.com

LIBRARY OF CONGRESS CATALOGING-IN-PUBLICATION DATA

Year round schools / Adriane Ruggiero, book editor.
   p. cm. -- (At issue)
  Includes bibliographical references and index.
ISBN-13: 978-0-7377-3791-2 (hardcover)
  ISBN-13: 978-0-7377-3792-9 (pbk.)
  1. Year-round schools--Juvenile literature. I. Ruggiero, Adriane.
LB3034.Y427 2008
  371.2'36--dc22
2007032862

ISBN-10: 0-7377-3791-3 (hardcover)
ISBN-10: 0-7377-3792-1 (pbk.)

Printed in the United States of America
10 9 8 7 6 5 4 3 2 1

Contents

Introduction

The changeover to year-round schools has grown in the United States over the past twenty years. Many of the school districts that have switched from a traditional school calendar with its nine weeks of summer vacation to a modified calendar built around several shorter vacations spread over the year do so because they need to raise student achievement levels in low-performing schools or in schools with low-income, minority, and/or non-English-speaking students. By reconfiguring the calendar to eliminate the long summer break they can increase instruction time and hopefully raise student achievement levels. Many other educators regard year-round schooling as a reform whose time has come, however. They not only see the benefits of a modified calendar for at-risk students but for *all* students who experience the same learning loss that occurs between the end of school in May or June and the start of school in August or September.

How do schools increase instruction time and also make sure students have breaks and vacations? Many educators who are involved in year-round schools propose several shorter vacations between two to four weeks in length spread over the year. In the vocabulary of year-round schooling these breaks are called *intersessions*. School principals currently operating under modified school calendars believe that intersessions are the key ingredient in measuring the success of a modified school calendar. According to Shelly Gismondi Haser and Ilham Nasser in their book, *Year Round Education: Change and Choice for Schools and Teachers*, the schools' ability to initiate and carry out creative intersession programs is directly linked to their basic mission of providing more in-school learning time for students.

Naturally, intersession breaks can serve as real vacations during which teachers and students use their time off to take trips, spend it with family and friends, or just decompress from the stresses of school. But for many school districts that have modified their school calendar, intersessions are a time for them to focus on raising student achievement levels. During intersessions, students receive extra help in subjects where they are below achievement levels (usually in reading or math at the elementary level), prepare to take state-wide tests, or receive enrichment in subject areas within the core academic areas of math, English, social studies, and science. Enrichment also includes a diverse array of cultural, athletic, and artistic opportunities, sometimes held off-campus. At the high school level, intersessions are more intensely focused on helping students increase their skills and knowledge in core academics and prepare for SATs. Many high school enrichment programs are obviously geared to preparing students for college-level work and broadening their fields of knowledge.

Intersession programs are usually not mandatory, but many schools that receive federal Title 1 funds encourage their usually low-income, non-native English-speaking students to attend the programs to receive remedial work and get on level as soon as possible. Schools usually charge students a small fee (usually for materials) for the intersession programs and can apply for state and federal funds and grant money to help defray the costs. Most importantly, intersessions are not "fluff" and involve a full school day during which students are transported back and forth to school, are given lunch and sometimes breakfast, and are often provided with after school care. Running successful intersession programs entails a great deal of work and coordination on the part of the school and the teachers. Each enrichment program, be it music appreciation, writing workshop, or environmental science, must be based on state curriculum guidelines and standards of learning and is required to have an outline, lessons plans, and a testing component.

Careful planning is an integral part of running intersessions, so much so that many year-round schools hire intersession coordinators and volunteers to carry out the work. Planning has to take place at least one year ahead of the actual start date of the intersession. Intersession coordinators use this time to survey students, develop courses based on student interests, line up instructors, buy supplies, arrange for student transportation, and send out newsletters to the community and parents about upcoming programs. The time is also spent interviewing potential instructors and signing them up to teach a course.

The backgrounds of the intersession teachers can help make the programs interesting and exciting. Retired teachers often serve as a pool of instructors for intersession programs. Some schools call upon professors or graduate students at local universities to teach intersession programs. Others recruit people from the community to teach. Those teachers who take part in intersession programs are paid for their time, one of the major reasons for their participation. But many teachers like teaching intersession programs for other than monetary reasons: they want to give extra help to the students, want to teach a different subject or a different grade level, or are just excited about sharing their knowledge of a language, skill or hobby. Teaching an intersession program also provides veteran and new teachers the opportunity to engage in more hands-on, non-traditional teaching methods such as team teaching or co-teaching. Teachers who do not take part in intersession programs also benefit by the breaks in the school calendar. Many appreciate the two- or four-week breaks as a time to plan their classroom instruction and coordinate with colleagues. Others use the intersession time to study in their subject area, read professional literature, or do course work for advanced degrees. Many others use the time to attend to their own families.

A feeling of professional accomplishment that comes from running intersessions is one of the biggest payoffs for teachers and schools. According to Darla DeVille, head of Star of the Sea School in Honolulu, Hawaii and quoted by Paul S. Piper in his Internet article *Year-Round Schools: the Star of the Sea Model*, "intersession classes impact support staff by increasing work flow, particularly with regard to the organization, registration, and accounting required by intersession classes. But it is that very work and commitment that gives the school community a sense of ownership and pride in their school."

1

Revising the Current School Calendar Has Many Implications

Elena Silva

Elena Silva is a senior policy analyst at Education Sector, an independent think tank focused on finding new solutions to the nation's most challenging educational problems.

Schools are experimenting with extending the amount of time students spend in the classroom. They have several reasons for embarking on this approach: to raise student achievement levels, meet federal standards, and be accountable to their state's education systems. But adding to the number of hours students actually spend involved in instruction does not necessarily mean students will learn more. Quality is more important than quantity in this case, and exceptional teaching does make a huge difference in the learning capabilities of students, especially those from low-income families. Studies show that students from low-income families benefit most from an extended-school day and their parents generally favor the concept. But selling the idea to other groups is difficult. Cost is an issue, as is the potential for student and teacher burn-out. Certain industries, such as the tourism industry, oppose changes in the school calendar, as do some parent groups. What is really needed in our schools is not more time but better quality teaching time, a restructuring of the curriculum to meet student needs, and a reinvigoration of core academics while not sacrificing other subjects.

The logic of time reform is simple—more time in school should result in more learning and better student performance. But this seemingly straightforward calculation is more complex than it appears. Research reveals a complicated relationship between time and learning and suggests that improving the quality of instructional time is at least as important as increasing the quantity of time in school. It also suggests that the addition of high-quality teaching time is of particular benefit to certain groups of students, such as low-income students and others who have little opportunity for learning outside of school.

What's more, the politics and cost of extending time make the reform a tough sell. Additional days and hours are expensive, and changing the school schedule affects not only students and teachers, but parents, employers and a wide range of industries that are dependent on the traditional school day and year. It is critical that policymakers understand the educational and political complexities of time reform before they attempt to extend the school year or take up other time–reform initiatives. . . .

The Changing School Calendar

Time in school has been added and subtracted in many ways throughout our country's history, although not always for obvious reasons. School schedules varied considerably by locality early in our country's history with some schools open nearly year round and others open only intermittently.

In large cities, long school calendars were not uncommon during the 19th century. In 1840, the school systems in Buffalo, Detroit, and Philadelphia were open between 251 and 260 days of the year. New York City schools were open nearly year round during that period, with only a three-week break in August. This break was gradually extended, mostly as a result of an emerging elite class of families who sought to escape the oppressive summer heat of the city and who advocated that children needed to "rest their minds." By 1889, many cities had moved to observe the two-month summer holiday of July and August.

Not all time in school is equal. . .

Rural communities generally had the shortest calendars, designed to allow children to assist with family farm work, but they began to extend their school hours and calendars as the urban schools shortened theirs. By 1900, the nation's schools were open an average of 144 days, but, with many youth in the workforce and few compulsory attendance laws for school, students attended an average of only 99 of those days.

School schedules underwent more adjustment during the 20th century to accommodate a changing population and the needs of war. Summer sessions were provided in some communities to teach English to immigrant students or to provide accelerated programs to allow students to graduate early, but most programs were used to manage a growing youth population and prepare a workforce. The first extended-day schools came into being during World War II to provide care for the school-aged children of women pressed into work.

By the 1960s, most schools in the country had settled on a schedule of 170–180 days, five days a week, six and a half hours a day. This has remained the standard in American public schools since then: a 2004 survey by the Council of Chief States School Officers found that 35 states require the school year to be 180 days or longer, and six require between 175 and 179 days; the same survey found 34 states require five or more instructional hours per day (or no less than 900 hours per year).

But today, as educators face unprecedented pressures to raise student achievement, the standard school day and school year are being reconsidered nationwide. . . .

Not All Time in School Is Equal

Not all time in school is equal because not all school and classroom time is devoted to formal instruction or learning. Time is spent on lunch, assemblies, walking between classes, announcements, and the many other things that go on in school. One can think of school time as being comprised of four different "types" of time, . . . The largest is *allocated school time*, followed by *allocated class time, instructional time*, and *academic learning time*. Allocated school time and allocated class time are the hours that students are required to be in school and class, but include recess, announcements, and the other non-instructional activities. Instructional time is the time devoted to formal instruction or learning, although much of that time may be lost to poor quality teaching and student inattention. Academic learning time is the time in which students are actually engaged in learning.

Any extended time proposals must focus on expanding the right kind of time. . .

While the distinctions may seem obvious, they are important because they make clear why any extended-time proposal must focus on providing the right kind of time, i.e., instructional time and academic learning time, rather than just adding hours in general. As would be expected, the research shows that the correlation between time and student achievement gets stronger with more engaged time. Students who are given more *allocated school time* have outcomes only slightly better than students who receive less. But the correlation between time and achievement increases when students are given more *instructional time*, and it is even greater when students' *academic learning time* increases. . . .

Clearly, any extended time proposals must focus on expanding the right kind of time—time when students are engaged in productive learning. Adding more hours would ostensibly provide more time for everything that occurs in schools, and in the best schools there would be an ample increase in academic learning time. But in poorly managed schools with inexperienced teachers and a host of other challenges, it is likely that more time would be lost to other activities.

"Schools that have strong leadership and are already on a trajectory of school improvement are most capable of making use of extended time in ways that will support student learning," says Jennifer Davis, president of Massachusetts 2020, a nonprofit organization leading the movement to extend school time in Massachusetts. In a 2005 study of eight successful extended-time schools, *Time for a Change: The Promise of Extended Time Schools for Promoting Student Achievement*, the organization found that extended time was an essential part of the schools' success, but other factors were also important, including strong leaders, excellent teachers, high student expectations, careful monitoring of performance, and a safe, supportive, and nurturing school environment. In other words, time was not an add-on in the schools, but part of a larger, coherent reform plan. . . .

Extended Time and the Flow of Learning

Extending and improving the use of instructional time could undoubtedly benefit all students. But studies suggest that extended time may matter more for some students than others. Poor and minority students are less likely than their more affluent peers to have educational resources outside of school and therefore may benefit more from increased school time.

Time's potential as a reform depends largely on whether the time is used effectively . . .

Evidence from the *Beginning School Study* (BSS), a longitudinal study begun in 1982 by sociologists Doris Entwisle and Karl Alexander, shows that lower-income children lose ground to higher-income children over time because of what researchers call summer learning loss. Children in middle-class and affluent families, researchers explain, continue to experience learning opportunities while they are out of school in the summer, but children from low-income families do not have the same opportunities and make virtually no learning gains during time off. Their "faucet theory" postulates that school provides a steady flow of learning opportunity for all children during the school year; the flow stops for low-income children when school is out, but continues for higher-income students who are provided learning opportunities elsewhere. Higher-income children in effect are getting more educational time through informal out-of-school summer opportunities. Therefore, differences in family background will inevitably lead to unequal gains for students unless other sources of learning are provided to make up for the summer deficit. . . .

Year-round school designs, which are also being looked at in time reform efforts, may reduce the negative effects of summer learning loss by eliminating the long summer vacation, but such proposals do not always target the students most in need of increased learning time. They also do not usually increase the absolute number of hours of school, but instead reorganize school schedules throughout the year, often to accommodate more students in the same facility. . . .

Increasing in-school time and providing out-of-school programs for the neediest students seems to help address the problems of summer learning loss and achievement gaps. Education organizations such as the Knowledge Is Power Program (KIPP) and Edison Schools, Inc. are examples of entities that extend in-school time. Students in KIPP, a network of public schools—mostly charters—in low-income communities, spend at least 50 percent more time in school than their peers attending regular public schools and show strong academic gains; KIPP lists "more time" as one of its five operating principles. A recent evaluation of KIPP schools in California credited KIPP's longer hours for its success, but also attributed it to other factors, including a strong culture of academic achievement, rigorous classes, and strict discipline. . . .

The Challenges of Extending School Time

Some strategies for extending time for learning have proved to be more beneficial than others, but all have attendant costs and complications. The financial investment needed to extend time is undeniably high and has thwarted many efforts. Most calculations suggest that a 10 percent increase in time would require a 6 to 7 percent increase in cost. The recent Massachusetts plan, which increased school time by 30 percent in its first year, required an additional 20 percent in base funding, or an average of $1,300 extra per student.

Cost calculations are based largely on increased school staffing, but often do not consider other costs such as those for additional building maintenance; electricity, telephone and other utilities; transportation; supplementary curricular materials; or for upgrading or modifying school facilities, many of which do not have appropriate lighting for early or late hours or air conditioning for summer months. These costs are harder to estimate, but are sure to raise the price of extending time.

The recent proposal by Minnesota school superintendents to extend the school year by 25 days (from 175 to 200) was estimated to cost $750 million dollars, which the superintendents determined was not feasible, either financially or politically.

But not all proposals are as expensive. Extending the school year, for example, is generally more costly than extending the school day. Keeping a school open for an extra hour or two will not generate any major new costs for transportation, building maintenance and utilities. Staff costs, too, are cheaper if hours rather than whole days are added. . . .

The extended-school model of KIPP receives most of its funding from state and local per pupil expenditures, but it also relies on other sources of funding to cover the costs of additional school time. The need varies depending on the location of the schools. California, for example, is proving to be a difficult place to operate KIPP schools because low state per pupil funding simply cannot cover the costs of higher teacher salaries and expensive real estate, and budgeted expenses per pupil often exceed the amount allocated. KIPP teachers typically make 20 percent more than traditional public school teachers for the extra time. To cover these costs, KIPP relies on fundraising at the school and national level, from car washes to private foundation support and federal appropriations.

The financial investment needed to extend time is undeniably high and has thwarted many efforts.

Strongest Opposition to Extended School

Another challenge is wide-ranging effects of changing school schedules. Altering school schedules impinges on more than students and teachers. The strongest opposition to extending school into the summer or throughout the year comes from middle-class and affluent parents who see no real benefit for their own children for giving up the vacation schedule they have come to expect. Also, entire industries—transportation, child care, food service—have been designed to align with current school schedules. Tourism and camping industries vigorously oppose school-time reform proposals, predicting financial losses if summer vacation is reduced. Resort and restaurant owners worry that more school in summer will mean fewer young people to hire for their businesses. And states and districts that rely on summer tourism for revenue are also wary of shorter summers. As a result, many states have proposed legislation to mandate that school start dates are no earlier than the week before Labor Day. Virginia districts must apply for waivers from the state school board to start school before Labor Day, a start date set by a state policy now known as the "Kings Dominion law," named after the popular theme park in the state that backed the 1986 legislation that keeps families vacationing through August and early September. . . .

Teachers' schedules are another important piece of any extended-time puzzle. Teachers unions want to ensure that their members will be fully compensated for extra time and that extended time schedules are voluntary. Although many teachers seem to support extended time for additional money, others see an extended work schedule as a real burden. Many teachers choose the profession because it offers a schedule that works for the rest of their lives. Teachers not only value afternoon hours and summer months to spend with and care for their own children, but also rely on this time to take professional-development courses. . . .

No Certain Benefit in Extending Time in Schools

John Hodge Jones, the former chair of the National Education Commission on Time and Learning and a former school superintendent, proclaimed that real education reform would not be possible until we have "revolutionized" the school day and year. Jones is right that time is a potentially important element of school improvement. Certainly, the current emphasis on accountability and assessment makes the effective management of school time more important than ever.

But education reform, certainly reform that is *revolutionary*, cannot be boiled down to just the minutes, hours and weeks of the school calendar. Schools, say [authors] Aronson, Zimmerman, and Carlos, must set high standards while gearing curriculum and instruction to students' skill levels, and engage students "so they will return day after day and build on what they have learned." They write:

> What matters most are those catalytic moments when students are absorbed in instructional activities that are adequately challenging, yet allow them to experience success. . . . Only when time is used more effectively will adding more of it begin to result in improved learning outcomes.

Time's potential as a reform depends largely on whether the time is used effectively and on its use as a resource to serve students most in need of extra learning opportunities, both inside and outside of school. Research shows that extending the right kind of time to the students who need it most can improve student learning and effectively close achievement gaps between poor and minority students and their more affluent peers. It can also enhance the rigor and relevance of a school's curriculum by providing more time for core academic subjects without sacrificing other subjects. And it can improve teaching by providing opportunities for teacher planning, collaboration and professional development. But the preponderance of evidence on extending time in schools suggests that the benefits of adding time to the school day or year are by no means certain or universal.

2

Year-Round Schooling Offers Benefits Over a Traditional Calendar

Charles Ballinger and Carolyn Kneese

Charles Ballinger is the executive director of the National Association for Year-Round Education. Carolyn Kneese is a former associate professor of educational administration at Texas A&M University–Commerce.

Year-round schooling enhances student learning because the learning is not interrupted by a long summer break during which, many experts say, students forget what they learned during the regular school year. That summer break is a remnant of an agrarian past when children were needed to work on farms. Today, student learning need not be dictated by season since learning goes on all the time. Many educators who teach in schools with modified or balanced calendars note that students are less likely to forget the knowledge they acquired because they experience fewer interruptions in instruction. However, students in these schools are actually in school the same number of days as students in schools with so-called traditional calendars. Instead of a three-month vacation in the summer, modified or balanced school schedules are built around several shorter breaks called intersessions. These breaks are spaced throughout the year and provide students with valuable opportunities for remedial work and advanced enrichment. For example, a school following a modified calendar might have 45 days of classes followed by a 15-day intersession. Both students and teachers experience less burnout under this system.

The National Educational Commission on Time and Learning has acknowledged what most educators instinctively know, but seldom give voice to: There is a disconnect between the way that students learn and forget and the currently-used school calendar, which has little relationship to that understanding. Since students can learn in all seasons and months of the year, educators and others might well consider whether or not a school calendar that is more closely aligned to student learning modalities can be developed.

The Issue of the School Calendar

The traditional school calendar is not primarily a learning calendar now, nor was it designed to be. Rather, it is an amalgam of responses to the economic and social needs of a nation both rural and urban. Original intents—to provide helping hands on the farms and ranches of a bygone era, to provide extended instruction in English for young European immigrants, or to offer special interest classes to children of wealthy urbanites—have long since been surpassed by events in the 20th and early 21st centuries.

Nevertheless, the traditional calendar persists in a majority of American schools. Buttressed by the strong force of doing things the way they have always been done and supported by the inertia of simply accepting what is and has been, the traditional calendar continues to be anchored, though rusting, in many communities. The policy issue that remains, however, is whether or not calendar stability is of a higher value than adoption of a new calendar designed to aid student learning.

Today considerable flexibility exists for creating time models that better serve students' educational needs. For example, almost all state legislatures require students to attend school fewer than half of the days each year (180 of 365). If schools were to publish and distribute a hypothetical calendar that alternated legislatively required in-school days (180) with out-of-school days (185), most members of the public would be astonished to realize that American students would be out of school every other day of the year! Viewed through this lens, it is quite clear that American students have not been asked, nor required, to make the time commitment to learning that other leading nations of the world have asked of their students.

A balanced year-round calendar provides a logical pacing of instruction, followed by regular breaks. Refreshed by the breaks, teachers and students return ready to work . . .

With significant learning loss occurring year after year because of the traditional long summer vacation, which in turn requires substantial time each autumn for reteaching the previous year's lessons. American students are not reaching the goals and expectations of the larger society. They are not likely to meet them when, as the commissioners of the National Education Commission on Time and Learning wrote, time usage in school virtually assures the failure of many students. Consequently, a question to be posed is this: Of what value is there to a community of having most of its classrooms unused for fully 25% of the possible school days each year. When America's students need more, rather than less, education?

While some educational authorities have suggested summer school as a solution to reduce summer learning loss, others respond that it is well to remember that considerably fewer than half of American students are involved in structured summer learning programs of any kind, including non-school activities. Further, they point out, the American summer school, for the most part, is not well-connected to the school's ongoing curriculum, lacking sufficient focus to be of much remedial help.

Other educators believe that summer remedial instruction comes too late to be useful. For example, if a student misunderstands an algorithm in October, he will most likely have to wait until the following June for the remediation process to begin. That struggling student's seven months of frustration, waiting for help, is hardly an energized prelude to successful summer remediation.

Summer Learning Loss

Now that educational research has verified what experienced teachers have known for decades—that students forget a considerable amount of information over the long summer—a pertinent question to be raised in each community is this: How long should a summer vacation be? Three weeks or four? Five or six? As long as 10 or 12? Summer learning loss is a significant policy issue that requires ongoing community consideration of how best to lessen the loss. A community's focus on that loss and its ramifications may well lead to calendar reformation.

Yet, to a larger extent than one might think possible, there are communities across the nation that have resisted even minimal consideration and discussion of summer loss. In those communities mere mention of summer loss is dismissed without an articulated rationale for the status quo other than it has always been that way.

To a certain extent, the notion of learning loss seemingly fades with the resumption of school each autumn. Rather than learning loss disappearing, however, its reality is simply camouflaged by the resumption of school. Summer loss accumulates over time. Eventually, students from disadvantaged homes—known to be especially vulnerable to summer loss— slip further behind their peers each year and increasingly struggle to catch up with other students, prompting them to eventually abandon school by dropping out.

Unfortunately, even some educators are reluctant to confront the seriousness of summer loss. . . . To raise the issue is to disturb the comfortable status quo. Without a political groundswell in the community to confront learning loss—a groundswell unlikely without raising the issue in the first place—there is little incentive to tackle the summer loss phenomenon. Most school board members and district administrators feel quite safe in accepting the status quo because they are keenly aware that the parents of the students most seriously hurt by summer loss are also the ones least likely to demand change. Nevertheless, if learning challenges and objectives set by state and federal governments are to be met, discussion in the community about calendar reform is overdue.

Some Reasons For Changing the School Calendar

Community discussions on calendar modification to date have generated six generalized reasons to change the calendar. The reasons follow.

1. *Modified, balanced calendars can effectively maintain student interest in learning.* Periods of teacher/student interaction in the classroom, followed by scheduled vacations, is a balanced way of learning. Interest remains high throughout the learning period because students can, in their more difficult moments, contemplate a vacation just a short time away. The vacation period, however, is not so long that students seriously lose skills previously taught. A balanced year-round-calendar provides a logical pacing of instruction, followed by regular breaks. Refreshed by the breaks, teachers and students return ready to work. Students thus learn to pursue work intensively, to rest and regenerate during short vacations, and then to work diligently again—a rhythm more like real life.

In contrast, the traditional school calendar begins its year after a nearly 3-month layoff. It lurches through the year by almost, but not quite, finishing the first semester before a two-week winter holiday period. The semester resumes for just three weeks after the holidays and then is completed. Once the first semester ends, teachers typically are given two or three days to grade semester final exams, record the grades, and plan—with negligible time available for thoughtful revision—the beginning of the second term.

Intersession ... is a fertile period for enrichment and creativity ...

The second semester has its quirks as well. Teachers, staff, and students begin the semester with a rush. A short spring break of one week or less is scheduled about halfway through the semester. After the break there is a long slide in student interest in learning as the student contemplates the long summer vacation ahead.

2. *Students, learning differently, require different time configurations.* While affirming this truism in both community forums and educational seminars, many educators and community leaders actually adhere to another quite opposite learning principle when it comes to the school calendar. In practice, these educational leaders subscribe to the thesis that all students learn in the same way, at the same time, and that one calendar fits all. Further, there is often a clear pattern of denial about summer learning loss. Consequently, these school leaders ignore the warning of the National Education Commission on Time and Learning that there is an unacknowledged design flaw in school time schedules that can be corrected with provisions of time options for learning.

3. *Intersession classes provide faster remediation and advanced enrichment.* After several weeks of class work in modified-calendar schools, students have a scheduled vaca-

tion—the length of time of which depends on local calendar choices. The vacation is called *intersession*, during which remediation can occur or enrichment can be offered. If an elementary student is struggling with fractions, or a secondary student with algebra, intersession becomes a welcomed opportunity to take immediate corrective action. If the action is successful, struggling students have the opportunity to resume class work at a level comparable to that of their classmates when instruction begins anew.

Intersession also is a fertile period for enrichment and creativity. Year-round schools have developed exciting 1- to 3-week classes in the arts, sciences, computers, and independent study units, as well as the standard basic subjects. Once parents understand the possibilities inherent in intersession learning units, they tend to support calendar change all the more readily.

4. *Students learning a second language can benefit the balanced calendar.* Students are arriving at schools with more diverse backgrounds than ever before. Consequently, a greater variety of languages is brought from the home to the school. A long summer away from language instruction is not helpful to students learning English as a second language. Indeed, the absence of formal language instruction is not helpful to any student learning a second language. Improving the school calendar can make a great difference in language acquisition for these students.

5. *Cocurricular and extracurricular activities can take place throughout the year and can reinforce previous learning.* Research indicates that students remember most when they have an opportunity to apply what they have learned. A modification of the school calendar, with its intersession periods, can allow students creative avenues to apply recent learning. For example, intersession programs that incorporate in-depth sci-

ence projects, independent science study, or science camp can add to what students have learned previously in their science classes.

The single-track's schedule is flexible enough that staff and parents can include an extra day or two, or an extra week, around legal holidays to take advantage of lower traveling costs or more quality family time . . .

Intersession intervals can also be excellent times to prepare for music events. Scholastic Aptitude Test (SAT) or American College Test (ACT) exams, or academic decathlons. For high school students, fall and winter intersessions can be desirable times to visit prospective college campuses. Student athletes can utilize intersession in at least two ways: 1) a significant portion of the sport's season is free of exam and homework requirements, allowing increased concentration on the sport: and 2) student athletes experiencing academic difficulty can use the intersession to correct the problem and retrieve good standing.

6. *Teachers can take advantage of year-long opportunities for staff development.* In a balanced calendar school, staff development is continuous and available throughout the year rather than available largely in the summer months. This in-service schedule is similar to that in professional fields such as medicine, law, and engineering.

Teachers' fears that an alternative calendar will prohibit them from pursuing advanced degrees have not been realized. Graduate schools live by the law of supply and demand. When teachers need in-service or graduate training, universities provide it. In areas where several teacher institutions vie for graduate students, the institutions compete vigorously to provide classes at times convenient to teachers.

A Single Track Calendar
and the Way It Works

Schools that choose to move to a single-track, balanced calendar generally do so with high purpose. They want to reduce—not eliminate—the long summer vacation of the traditional calendar to reduce the forgetting that accompanies it. They also want to establish to a greater degree than heretofore possible a school calendar that mirrors the way students learn: continuously. Thus, they adopt a single-track calendar in which all students and teachers follow the same schedule, but one in which there are periods of learning followed by periods of vacation (called intersessions).

Schools considering calendar modification for learning reasons only have the luxury of choosing among many schedules, unlike those schools facing or experiencing heavy overenrollment. The former may choose among a variety of structured calendars such as 45/15, 60/20, 60/15, 90/30, or variations of these common four. They also have the opportunity to develop and implement a design of instructional delivery of their choice: quarter, semester, trimester, or continuous. In those schools favoring a philosophy of meeting student needs by personalizing instruction, parents and students may choose among personalized calendars, which are designed to respond specifically to individual student needs and parental schedule(s).

The single-track's schedule is flexible enough that staff and parents can include an extra day or two, or an extra week, around legal holidays to take advantage of lower traveling costs or more quality family time. There can also be consideration of special days set aside for community festivals, local events, and county fairs, all within the context of vacations no longer than eight weeks and most no longer than six weeks.

There are other reasons to consider implementation of single-track, balanced calendars. Utilizing scheduled vacation periods of three to five weeks, classroom teachers have time to reflect upon what has previously transpired in the teacher/ student interaction and to plan future instructional strategy.

Because of the intermittent, scheduled vacations, there is reduced teacher and student burnout. For both, there is a period away from classroom tensions and personality conflicts that are so often present when humans interact. Because of this period of recuperation, some single-track schools have reported better attendance on the part of both teachers and students. Other schools have reported fewer student disciplinary referrals, which they attribute to the scheduled vacation intervals and the opportunity to dampen negative feelings toward the school on the part of some students.

Concerns of Parents and Others About Change

At the same public forums that generated reasons to implement a single-track modified calendar, there were reasons offered not to proceed with modification. Eight of those reasons are reviewed here. Three are linked to issues of family life, three are linked to school district administrative or operational concerns, and two are linked to non-school experiences. None of the eight are linked to instructional concerns.

All of these concerns are real to those who raised them. All have been addressed in other communities that have implemented a balanced calendar. All have been resolved or rendered non-threatening to the satisfaction of most families.

Parents were initially concerned about possibly having their children on differing schedules, if, for example, the local elementary school were to move to a modified calendar plan, while the feeder high school remained on a traditional schedule. Likewise, parents raised the matter of family vacations if calendar change were to occur. Both of these concerns have been, and can be, ameliorated to a large degree by printing and distributing to parents well in advance both the modified and traditional calendars. Parents quickly realize that there is a common in-school schedule most of the year and that there are usually four to six weeks of common vacation time in the summer, two weeks at Christmas/New Year's, and one week in common during spring vacation. That is a total of seven to nine weeks of common vacation each year. Since most families rarely take more than three weeks of vacation time together annually, including the winter holidays, this issue of separate schedules ceases to be a major one.

Parents were also concerned about whether or not child care would be available when students were on their scheduled vacations/intersessions. Experience in other communities has shown that child care is a service responsive to parental needs and follows the law of supply and demand. If child care organizations do not offer service at the times parents demand it, the organizations quickly go out of business. Thus, when the school schedule changes, the child care schedule follows quickly.

Parents also wondered whether or not students could still find and hold jobs after calendar modification. Concerns about student employment are usually allayed by the experiences over the past three decades of high school students in modified calendar schools. A pertinent fact for consideration is that the vast majority of high school students do not have jobs affected by a change in the school schedule. For example, only on occasion do freshmen and sophomores have work especially sensitive to calendar change, if indeed they hold jobs at all. Even among 16- to 18-year-olds it is not common to have a job affected by calendar change.

Students holding jobs have actually been helped by balancing the calendar. Most employment of high school students is in the fast food, grocery, and service industries, jobs which are usually part-time and available in all months and seasons of the year. Because of the nature of these jobs, experience has shown that students in modified-calendar high schools are available to work in the above businesses at times when other high school and college students are in class and not available. By not having to compete with every other high school and college student for all-too-few jobs in the summer, modified-calendar students do very well indeed during their several vacation periods.

There is one job-related circumstance that merits special attention. Organized opposition to calendar change in some communities has come from the summer recreation industry. Fearful that minimum-wage labor will not be available at certain peak times, the industry has suggested to parents and others that a community's economy will be greatly damaged if minimum-wage labor is not available and local resort businesses fail.

This perceived threat to summer recreation sites can be viewed two ways. On the one hand, local summer resorts pay taxes, which is the lifeblood of all government agencies, including public schools. Consequently, no harm to business is wanted nor intended when a school changes its calendar. Rather, modification of a calendar is activated to attain the purpose of schools, which is to help students achieve the highest degree of learning possible. That is what taxpayers, including summer resorts, expect for their money. School districts in resort communities should work with local businesses to determine the number of students, if any, needed for successful business operations. It may well be that a summer vacation of six to eight weeks may provide ample workers during the peak season. Work/study programs may supplement resort personnel needs. Discussion should include whether the resort(s) will be employing college or high school students, and if the latter, whether any will be below the age of 18.

On the other hand, the active opposition to calendar modification by the summer recreation industry is mystifying to many, since 99.9% of America's K-12 students are not employed nor eligible to be employed by this industry. Is it sound public policy to respond solely to the 0.1% that may be employed in the summer recreation industry, at the expense of the 99.9% who are not?

Parents also worried whether or not their children could be involved in activities such as Little League or high school sports. Activities such as these continue as before, experience has shown. They are affected little to none by balancing the calendar.

Other Stated Concerns

Other stated concerns revolved around air-conditioning during warm weather, building cleaning and maintenance, and having some schools out of sync with others in the district on such circumstances as teacher in-service and graduate work.

School administrative and operational challenges are easily taken care of in the single-track format. Maintenance and cleaning of school facilities continue as before. Since there are several scheduled vacations each year, maintenance and deep cleaning are actually enhanced by the single-track arrangement. No longer do the school facilities need to wait until summer for cleaning and maintenance.

Air-conditioning of any school functioning in all seasons of the year is an ongoing discussion with educational, physical, and financial implications far broader than first realized. If students cannot learn because of heat in a non-air-conditioned school, then is the value of classes held in May, June, and September suspect, as well as any summer classes held in that school? Yet hundreds of non-air-conditioned schools hold classes in warm weather each year. On the other hand, if students can learn in summer school despite the heat, then why would they not learn in a year-round school as well?

Most schools built in the past 20 years are built with air-conditioning in mind. Many older schools have been wholly or partially air-conditioned in the past two decades. Over time, this issue will dissipate as more schools move into some kind of climate control. In the meantime, balancing of the school calendar should be approached on its own merits first in a community's discussion, and once that decision is affirmed, then additional consideration can be given to climate control in the classroom.

The content of teacher in-service does not change because of a change in a school's schedule. The timing of the in-service may change in those districts that offer two or more calendar options to students and parents; however, districts offering a choice of calendars have found common times when all staff are available for in-servicing.

Reasons for Choosing a Multi-Track Schedule

As noted previously, a single-track year-round calendar is one in which a school, or a school district, functions on a schedule in which all students and school staff follow the same days in school and on vacation. Single-track calendars are adopted to provide a more balanced and enriched educational program, to reduce the reality of learning loss over the long summer vacation of the traditional calendar, to accommodate the needs of a particular community, or a combination of these. It is not intended to provide additional space, promote additional efficiency of resources, or to solve administrative or logistical problems.

Multi-track year-round education (YRE), on the other hand, is implemented to do what single-track does not do: provide additional capacity to house students, maximize the efficient use of resources, solve one or more administrative or logistical problems, or do a combination of these three. A multi-track schedule provides more classroom space by having a portion of the student body on vacation or "off-track" at any time during the year. It is one in which the instructional and vacation/intersession periods of each track (or group) are alternated throughout the entire year. Thus, not all enrolled students are in school on the same days. Multi-track calendars provide shorter vacation periods, as do single-track calendars, thus reducing forgetting and advancing student achievement. Nevertheless, the primary intention of implementing a multi-track schedule is to solve and rectify a prior problem, such as overcrowding. . . .

3

The Traditional School Calendar Can Continue to Work in the Future

Robin Lockett Carter

Robin Lockett Carter contributed research papers while a graduate student at the University of Alabama in Huntsville.

Changing the school calendar from a traditional one to a year-round schedule will do little to raise achievement levels for students. Student performance rests on many variables including the quality of the teachers, the involvement and support of parents, and who the students are as individuals. In addition, changing the school calendar to eliminate summer "learning loss" will not solve the problem of students not learning to remember. Studies show that it is very difficult to gauge student retention but many experts believe that students (and many adults) have trouble remembering in the short-term. Creative teachers can develop strategies for combating this problem and do so regardless of what the calendar says. One approach is to teach higher-level thinking skills rather than rote memorization. There is no concrete proof that year-round schooling raises student test scores of ability to retain information. If teachers, administrators, and communities agree on giving high priority to education, there will be no need for the "quick fix" of changing the school calendar. The traditional school calendar worked in the past and can continue to work in the future. The sources and material used for this article are from 1999, and may not accurately reflect current statistical trends in the United States school system.

Robin Lockett Carter, *Year-Round School: Not the Solution for Failing Schools*, Huntsville, AL: University of Alabama in Huntsville, 1999. Reproduced by permission. http://schoolyear.info/res_academic.html

When I was in high school during the early 1990s, our school system was considering making a change from the traditional school calendar to that of a year-round calendar. I remember being intrigued by the prospect of attending school throughout the year. I was always one of those students who bored easily, whether it was with school or vacation. Year-round schooling sounded like the perfect answer. I felt that by shortening both school and vacation times into sections, it would be a great solution to my short attention span problem. However, I was in the minority. Many of my friends disliked the idea citing summer jobs, summer camps, spring training for various sports as things they would miss out on if a year-round school program were to be implemented at our school. We were not basing our opinions on test score statistical data or on financial spreadsheets; we just knew what sounded good to us at the time.

Not a Solution to Learning Loss

As I look back on those years, I am glad a year-round calendar was never implemented. I now know that my boredom could have been solved with more extracurricular academic activities during the school year and with a job during the vacation periods. I cannot say for sure that a change in the calendar would not have made a difference in how much or how well I learned as a student. However, I feel that my performance, as well as many of my friends' performances, depended more on our parents, our teachers and most importantly on who we were as individual students. This idea, however, is not what the proponents for a year-round calendar would have you believe. It is my contention that a change in the school calendar and increased retention are not related by causation. Year round schooling cannot eliminate the problem of students not learning to remember. The purpose of this paper is to address both the advantages and disadvantages associated with year-round school calendars in hopes of showing that a calendar change is not the solution to a failing academic program.

The fundamental reason for the transition [from a traditional calendar to a year-round calendar] in most schools appears to be financial.

Before inundating the reader with the specifics of year-round schooling, it would be beneficial to discuss terminology. The term year-round school (YRS) is not synonymous with extended school. A year-round school program does not lengthen the academic calendar, it merely breaks it up into segments. . . . YRS can be strictly defined as a reorganization of the school year because it is designed to utilize the school facility during all four seasons. There are also many forms of year–round schooling. A school that adopts a YRS calendar also has the option of creating different tracks. Multi-tracking refers to the practice where there are two to four groups of students attending the same school, but at any one time during the school year, a different group would be on vacation. . . . This essentially creates different schools within the same building.

Arguments for YRS

There are many arguments for the implementation of year-round schooling. The basis for the decision by most schools to make the change to YRS is to alleviate overcrowding. . . . Multi-tracking can increase a school's capacity by as much as twenty-five percent because there would always be one-fourth of the student population on vacation. Therefore, the fundamental reason for the transition in most schools appears to be financial. However, it remains to be seen as to whether or not YRS can save money. In fact, a single-track YRS program can actually cost more than the traditional program. Single-track plans do not accommodate more students, there is more strain placed on the facilities because there is no true off-time and the school must stay in operation during one of the most expensive seasons of the year. . . . Using the school building during summer months adds another cost not usually incurred by traditional schools. It has been reported that the largest cost associated with preparing existing facilities for YRS is that of installing air conditioning. . . . Schools in Los Angeles recently voted to return to the traditional calendar after only three years of YRS, citing unbearable summer temperatures as one of the main reasons for their displeasure with the program. . . .

Retention is a difficult problem to gauge . . .

Costs of YRS

Increases in utilities cost are only one increase that should be expected, however. Additional costs in the form of extra staff, increased operating costs, maintenance downtime, increased teacher salaries, building upgrades, and additional transportation have all been reported by school systems that originally adopted YRS in hopes of saving money. . . . For example, Houston, Texas schools abandoned the YRS program after eight years because of the added expenses and no true relief from overcrowding or improvements in achievement. The predicted savings from reinstating the traditional calendar reached approximately seven million dollars. . . . One must wonder with all the extra expenses that would be incurred from implementing a YRS program if it would not be more feasible to build an entirely new school building. Over time, a new building may actually be a more cost-effective alternative for school systems seeking to relieve overcrowded buildings. . . .

Year-round schooling is not only touted to be a solution for overcrowding, but also a means for increasing student academic performance. While the majority of the schools making the transition to YRS admit that the driving force is to increase school capacity, an alternative claim has been that it decreases learning losses experienced over the long summer vacations. . . . The reduction in learning loss would, in theory, decrease the amount of review time needed at the beginning of each school year. . . . However, statistics to support this claim are inconclusive. One study that involved third and sixth grade students in San Diego, California, shows that students who attended school year-round outscored their traditional school counterparts in seventeen of twenty-seven areas on a basic skills test. . . . There are other schools like those in San Diego that report similar results and yet year-round education has not been consistently proven to have a positive or negative effect on academic retention or achievement. . . .

Short-Term Learning Loss

Retention is a difficult problem to gauge because assessments cannot separate retention from learning. It is an extremely arduous task to evaluate what students learn in a unit of time. Regardless of how retention is measured, many studies show that the greatest loss incurred by students, and adults alike, is that of short–term learning. It has been shown that a substantial loss occurs within an hour of instruction and the majority occurs within two or three weeks. . . . As a result, it seems only logical that by increasing the number of breaks throughout a school year, as YRS does, it would actually promote learning loss. As one Vermont middle school teacher commented, "Check out what happens to students' memories in the one week between Christmas and the New Year. Kids forget things every time school's out". . . . This would also tend to increase the amount of time needed to review because teachers would essentially have to restart the school year several times throughout the year. . . . However, the use of teaching strategies by capable teachers can decrease short-term learning loss regardless of the calendar. By teaching higher level thinking skills instead of inundating students with details, they could retain information long after their test taking days are over.

With no concrete evidence to show the contrary, implementing a year-round educational program seems to be a very expensive gamble.

Another argument in favor of year-round schooling is that it helps students whose first language is not English or otherwise at risk students. The apparent reason that a YRS program would aid these individuals is that the students would receive constant scholastic reinforcement throughout the school year. This reinforcement would probably not be received otherwise at home during the longer summer breaks associated with the traditional calendar. . . . While it is a valid point that returning English as a Second Language (ESL) students to their homes where they could possibly be bombarded with their native languages . . . , the question of aiding the minority at the expense of the majority remains. Perhaps voluntary, no-cost programs specializing in continual education for ESL students and their families could be implemented by communities that show a need for improvement in this area.

Teacher and Student Burnout

Opponents of year-round education can use some of the same studies and reports heralded by proponents to further their cause as well. Statistics can be molded to suit either side of the argument; however, there are some considerations that cannot be reflected with test scores and, as a result, are often over looked. Teacher and administrator burnout, for example, is a rampant occurrence in school systems that practice year round school. . . .

Many administrators find that they lose opportunities for self and teacher evaluation and planning. In multi-track YRS systems, there are usually only two weeks per year, as opposed to two months, where there are no students in school. . . . Other factors include the effects YRS could have on band or sports programs . . . , internal communication and course scheduling. . . . Less crucial, but still very valid problems could also arise as a result of YRS. Scheduling family vacations, summer employment for students and teachers who may need to supplement family income, arranging day care, dress codes for students attending school in the summer, and perhaps even seasonal tourist industries could all be greatly affected. . . .

Learning Is Complicated

The National Educational Commission on Time and Learning conducted research on the amount of time spent in school in the early 1990s. Their research alludes to the fact that learning is a complicated concept that is only partially attributed to time. While the commission recognized that American school children spend less time in classrooms than many other countries, they were unable to show a direct correlation between time and learning. . . . With no concrete evidence to show the contrary, implementing a year-round educational program seems to be a very expensive gamble. A calendar change could cause more turmoil than improvements in most situations. As with any program, complete dedication and solid communication is needed to make it a success. The existing school calendar has worked in the past and can continue to work in the future.

Until politicians, administrators, teachers, parents and students decide to make improving education a priority, there will always be alternative "quick fixes" that give the appearance of being a solution to the overall problem. We must get to the core of the problem in our schools by re-training teachers, involving parents and community leaders, and providing the best educational experience we can offer. This is a plan must be followed, regardless of the calendar.

4

Extended-Time Schools Benefit Students

Jennifer Davis

Jennifer Davis is co-founder and president of Massachusetts 2020, an organization that is working to reform the school calendar and extend the time students are in school.

The way American students are schooled must change if students are going to be able to compete in a global economy. Year-round schooling may not be enough to bring about this change. One way to reform our educational system is to change the school calendar and extend the number of hours and months students spend in school. In Massachusetts, the state government supports the efforts of school districts to extend the time students are in school and receiving instruction. These extended-time schools benefit students by providing them with additional time during the school day for mastery in core academics, for remediation in specific subject areas and for enrichment activities. Extended-time schools also benefit teachers by providing them with extra time for preparation. Parents also benefit from the extended-time schedule because it more closely matches their own work schedule.

At Massachusetts 2020—and now in districts throughout our state—we are pressing for a longer day and a longer year. That is, we seek students to be in school for more time, not just for the calendar to be re organized to eliminate the

Jennifer Davis, "The Promise of Extended-Time Schools for Closing the Achievement Gap: A Speech to the National Association of Year-Round Education," *Massachusetts 2020*, February 27–28, 2006, pp. 2–15. Reproduced by permission. www.nayre.org

long summer break which can act to interrupt—and therefore set back—learning. Although we applaud and support the efforts [of the National Association of Year Round Education (NAYRE)], we believe that the *additional* time during the day and year we are seeking will afford students and teachers more opportunities than they have in the current calendar of 180 six-hour days. In a longer day and year, students can become involved in enrichment activities which are integrated deeply into their learning in core academic subjects; teachers can have time for common planning and individual preparation time built into their days; and parents can be supported by making their child's school schedule match more closely with their own work schedule. We agree that the current summer vacation schedule can be a detriment to learning, but we also want to see children get *more* time in productive learning environments.

What led us to this conclusion was a simple fact, which you may already know. Children spend only 20 percent of their waking hours in school. That's it—20 percent. There is so much that takes place in the 80 percent of time they spend outside of school that has a profound impact on what they can learn and achieve and, yet, somehow, as a nation, we expect that 20 percent of time is sufficient to override or compensate for the other four-fifths of kids' time. This expectation is especially misplaced when talking about kids from economically disadvantaged backgrounds where they often lack the familial assets—both financial and otherwise—that can give them a leg up on school learning. Kids from poor neighborhoods are less likely to be involved in quality after-school activities, less likely to come from homes that have access to things needed to support learning—from private tutors to adequate books in the home—and more likely to confront barriers to learning like poor health and frequent moves. How can only one-fifth of any given student's life possibly make up for all the liabilities that a child may suffer from as a result of coming from a disadvantaged home?

The Impact of Giving Poor Kids More Time in School

As you may know, the best empirical research that shows the degree to which out-of-school factors influence school performance comes from scholars exploring the summer gap. One study by [researchers] Alexander, Entwisle and Olson tested two groups of students—one from middle-class families and one from poor families—in Fall and Spring in five successive years. Results showed that students of low and high socioeconomic status made essentially the same relative academic progress from Fall to Spring (that is, during the school year), but that the learning curve for students from low SES stayed flat (or declined) from Spring to Fall (over the summer), while those of high SES students continued to rise. The end result is that by the end of fifth grade, the overall gap between low SES students and high SES students had grown so that the students from poor families are approximately two grade levels behind in verbal and 1.5 years behind in math.

A longer school day and year will certainly not entirely overcome this gap, but more time, together with other essential elements that comprise a quality education, can tip the balance in favor of promoting academic achievement. We have seen first hand, in eight schools we visited over the 2004–05 school year, how the impact of more time cannot be underestimated. . . .

Mass 2020 reviewed education data from across the country and found that there was no single source in the U.S. that documented how more learning time actually impacted student learning outcomes. In fact, time as an element in learning was . . . almost tangential to the main research fields in learning. Certainly, little research has been done outside of controlled experiments to understand how more time makes a difference to a school and to the individual learning process. Neither was there any one source of information that identified states, districts or schools that had systematically added learning time to the schedule.

More time does not mean just more of the same—more time sitting in classrooms . . .

As such, Mass 2020 secured funding to investigate a set of high-performing schools that had actually increased the time spent learning by extending the school day and year to understand how such a practice was implemented and how the educators there perceived the additional time as facilitating their positive outcomes. Specifically, we chose to study eight extended-time schools that had already demonstrated success and also were serving populations that in traditional schools were lagging behind. (Incidentally, we defined an extended-time school as any school where all students attend for at least 15% more time than the surrounding district.) Our secondary expectation was that our findings might push policymakers and educators to think about how they could spread the benefits of extended time to a much greater number of schools.

We released our study back in November and I want to share with you key findings in four areas—scheduling for students, benefits for learning, staffing structure and financing. . . .

A Better Use of Time

I am going to dive in deep to each of the areas I mentioned a moment ago, but let me first give you the topline findings for each. First, on scheduling, more time does not mean just more of the same—more time sitting in classrooms. While there generally is some additional time devoted to core academics, there is also a large chunk of time set aside for enrichment activities (for example, arts, music and sports) and also the opportunity for many (if not all) students to receive individualized or small group tutoring. Second, for teachers, the extra time is generally perceived not as a burden of having to spend more time at school, but as a benefit—giving them opportunity to hone their craft and develop camaraderie with their colleagues. Third, financially, extended-time schools do cost more, but the increased costs do not rise nearly as fast as the time added because so much of the costs are leveraged. For instance, typically health care benefit or transportation costs do not go up when the day is lengthened by two hours. Finally, across the eight schools we visited, there was near universal appreciation of the value of more time for enabling the school to reach its potential. . . .

A longer day allows for longer individual classes . . .

These schools offered an average of 9 hours per week of enrichment. Most traditional schools offer 4 hours at the most. More time also offers more time for activities that might get squeezed like recess. In fact, there was one district in Massachusetts where the superintendent tried to eliminate recess in order to build in a few more minutes in class. Needless to say, the move caused an uproar among parents. The schools in our study never had to make that choice.

Benefits to Teaching and Learning

Beneath this overview analysis of student schedules, there are a few scheduling-related practices that are worth pointing out that, according to the teachers and administrators, benefit the teaching and learning process. The most obvious is that a longer day allows for longer individual classes. In addition to enabling more time on task, specifically, the elongated class periods has led some schools to re think the organization of entire curricula and, in some cases, use a much longer period to blend two curricula together. (For example, a two-hour humanities class for middle school students integrates skills learned through English like reading and writing into a social studies curriculum.) Beyond the effects on individual classes, more time built into a student's schedule facilitates the opportunity for an individual student to be pulled out of a non-core academic class for tutoring or, more common, for the school to designate times during the day when students receive homework help or individual or small group instruction. It also allows schools to build in many enrichment activities and, importantly, because all enrolled students are there for the additional hours, those activities can be placed anywhere in the day—not just in their traditional "after-school slot."

Of course, the real reason we care—or anybody cares—about an extended-time schedule is whether it makes a difference for the teaching and learning. In addition to the academic data, educators and students we spoke with at these schools, emphasized that more time definitely does have a real impact. First, with more time, there is definitely the ability to extend individual classes. This enables not only more time on task . . . it also enables teachers to cover more topics and topics more in-depth. One teacher we spoke with mentioned how much easier it is to teach a 90-minute class than a 50-minute one precisely because she was able to take longer to explain topics and longer for the students to work with and internalize the material. It also allows teachers to deal more effectively with diverse ability levels. One student argued that a longer class means no question is left unanswered.

The major cost driver at the school level for each additional hour is teacher salary increases.

It is worth noting, too, that like every other school, these schools feel the most pressure to reach proficiency in math and English, so they do give a bit more time to those two subject areas—all for the purpose of increasing learning time, deepening the curriculum, etc. But unlike in a traditional school, this extending of time in math and English does not mean that the schools have to steal time from science or social studies.

Enforcing Core Academics

The other major piece that these schools add, as I mentioned, is enrichment activities. Now these activities vary from things like arts, drama, sports and music to chess club to—for older kids—internships and community service. What they do, however, is excite kids about learning in ways that often a classroom can't. Because they are highly connected to what the kids are learning in school, it is not just "wasted time," but activities that truly enforce core academics. For example, one school had kids in art class working on making replicas of quilts using particular geometric designs used by the Underground Railroad during slavery. This art project had managed to reinforce both history and geometry in a single lesson.

Finally, the individual tutoring allows not only the benefits of more time on task, but also helps to deepen child-teacher relationships as the tutoring is typically conducted by the students' own teachers in either designated times or pull-out sessions throughout the day.

Now, we come to the issue of how to staff these schools. After all, if you increase the teacher work day from an average of 6 hours to one that is closer to 8 hours, the school will definitely need to think about how it can recruit and retain teachers for that model. We found that there were two basic arrangements. The first is practiced entirely by charter schools which, of course, are public schools with the flexibility to operate this way. Namely, that for teachers expecting to work a longer day, there is no supplemental compensation. Instead, these teachers claim that other benefits like a smaller class size or a supportive school culture make up for the fact that they might work longer hours. Yet, this obviously is not an arrangement that is all that useful outside of charter schools.

Regular districts which abide by union contracts can't expect to have teachers work more hours for the same pay. Instead, these teachers typically get either stipends or a set hourly rate beyond their base salary. In some cases, they simply get a percentage higher than their salary would be at a non-extended-time school.

In all of the schools we visited, there was use of supplementary staff, especially for enrichment activities. In some instances, these staff operated more as paraprofessionals and worked alongside teachers in the classrooms. In most cases, they operated their own classes around specialized topics like instrument lessons or karate. Often, the supplemental staff did more than just expand programming for students; it also freed up time for core academic teachers to meet in common planning sessions or participate in professional development activities. . . .

Financing Extended Time Schedules

Now let's move to the area of financing, the area that always seems to stand in the way of even beginning a discussion of restructuring the school calendar. As I noted earlier, the costs of these extended-time schools was more—in most cases—but the additional costs over what a standard school in the district would cost per pupil was not nearly as much as the amount of additional time added. . . .

The major cost driver at the school level for each additional hour is teacher salary increases. You don't have to pay more for the roof or the desks and chairs. There are modest increases in energy costs, of course, and other personnel, like secretaries and such, but most of costs to operate a school remain steady whether that school is in operation for six hours or eight hours. Each additional day added beyond the traditional year of 180 days does cost a bit more because of transportation costs, but still is far lower than the increase in total time. . . .

The other reason that extended-time schools cost less than the time they add is because—being innovative institutions—they find ways to leverage money that already comes in to them or obtain additional money than they receive through regular district, state and federal sources. They shift usage of grants, or apply for new money that can be used in a variety of ways. For example, many of the schools receive 21st Century Community Learning Center grants to pay for a coordinator who then coordinates all the partnerships in the school. These partners, in turn, often come with their own private grant money so they cost little or nothing for the school. The bottom line is that because these schools are breaking from the traditional, it takes some creativity and extra effort to make it work. We hope someday that extended-time schools will become the norm with the financing understood as a necessary part of a state and district budget.

Importance of Leadership

I need to raise an important point and one I made at the outset. Each of these extended-time schools has many more assets than just the additional time. In fact, the time itself is meaningless unless it can be utilized well. To make that happen, schools need a set of other building blocks. First and foremost, a school—like a business or any organization—needs a strong leader with vision and sound management skills to be successful. Successful principals are able to set high expectations for teachers and students; convey a compelling vision for the school's success; create a work environment for teachers that is stimulating, supportive, and rewarding; and leverage and attract resources to support the school's needs.

The principal sets the tone for the school and also focuses on developing other key elements, such as: building external partnerships; fostering a positive school culture; integrating the positive use of data within school operations; reaching out to and including families within the school; and, perhaps most importantly, building and enhancing a professional corps of teachers. All of these are necessary for success.

Now where does extended-time fit into all this? The schools we visited tell us that it is a tool—more time with students makes it easier to do their jobs and makes their work more effective. It is like flour and yeast in bread—you need both to yield the right result, but it is impossible to separate out the relative importance of each.

5

Extended-Time School Programs Pose Problems for Parents and Students

Philissa Cramer

Philissa Cramer writes for Advocates for Children, a not-for-profit organization comprised of parents, child advocates, teachers, journalists and others who work to improve public education in New York City.

Extended school-day programs promise to deliver educational remediation and enrichment for New York City's public school children. And many parents like the idea of the extra help their children receive. However, the extended school day impacts parents and children's work, transportation, and schedules in a negative way. Communication between the schools and parents break down so parents don't know their child's schedule or when he or she will be picked up by the school bus. In particular, single parents worry when transportation schedules change and they must make arrangements with their employers. As the school day is extended, some programs are eliminated as schedules are juggled. Instead of spending millions on changing the bus schedules, the scarce resources can be put to better use by adding extra teachers to reduce class sizes. Meanwhile, many students in schools with extended-day programs are burned out after a long day that leaves little time for rest, play or being with friends.

In a new Insideschools.org poll, three out of four parents said the citywide extended-school-day program affects their work, transportation, or after school plans. Some said their children's after school programs are being cancelled entirely, and others say their children are being forced to spend more time on school buses than ever before.

Starting this week, 290,000 of the city's 1.1 million students are required to attend 37 1/2-minute tutoring sessions, in groups of 10, before or after school. An additional 40,000 are invited to attend. For most other students, the school day was shortened by 10 minutes.

The poll, to which 319 Insideschools.org readers responded as of Feb. 6, reveals a breakdown in communication between schools and parents before a major mid-year change to schools' schedules. While the poll may not reflect a representative sample of parents, it does reflect wide spread concern with the schedule changes.

Of the respondents—more than 90 percent of whom are parents—half said they had received "inadequate" or no information about what will happen during the extra minutes, and about 30 percent said they had received insufficient information about the change itself.

And of the respondents who needed information about changes to their child's after school and bus schedules, 40 percent said they had not gotten any.

Logistical Problems

While many readers said they are looking forward to having their children receive extra help, others complained about the logistical impact of changing schedules mid-year. Only 27 percent of respondents said the change would not affect them, and most said they would feel pressure from the change on their work schedule (26 percent), after school plans (10 percent) and transportation plans (5 percent). Thirty-two percent of respondents said the extra session would have an impact in more than one of the categories. "I am a single parent and the sole supporter of my two children," wrote Maria Zemel, whose children attend PS 128 in the Bronx. "Having a school schedule change puts me in a very difficult situation with my employer."

You ask me if it [the extended-day session] is too long or too short, and I say both—too long for teachers who are putting in a full day, too long for mandated children . . . , too long for children who are not mandated but have to bide their time . . .

Several parents reported that their child's after school programs are being cut or threatened to make way for the new minutes. A respondent reported that at Louis Armstrong Middle School in Queens, "an elective 9th period has been scrapped," and parent Renate Eppich reports that the "excellent self-sustaining after school program" at PS 191 in Queens is being discontinued "until further notice." At PS 154 in Queens, the computer program and chorus are being dismantled, a parent wrote. In Brooklyn, the Project Boost program at IS 220 is also shutting down, wrote parent Theresa Basso.

Other parents expressed concern about the costs and timing of the new bus schedules. Parent Maureen Doran wrote that her daughter, who attends PS 153 in the Bronx, will now be picked up more than an hour before the school day begins and dropped off more than an hour after it ends, up from about 30 minutes before the change. Another parent wrote that the first bus schedule she was given ended up being revised, and as of Jan. 31, she still didn't know how transportation for her child would work.

Misdirecting Resources

Some parents said the high cost of changing bus schedules—which one parent said approaches half a million dollars at her school—suggests that the extended-day program misdirects scarce resources. "The extra money that will be spent to bus the children for two dismissal sessions could be better spent by adding extra teachers to reduce class size," wrote Stephen Pruden, whose daughter attends MS 158 in Queens.

Poll respondents were split between thinking the extra 37 1/2-minute session is "too long, because students and teachers are already in school long enough" (44 percent) and thinking it is "too short, because it will be too hectic for anything to get done" (39 percent). Just 18 percent of respondents said the length of the session is "just right." One parent wrote, "You ask if it is too long or too short, and I say both—too long for teachers who are already putting in a full day, too long for mandated children who are burned out by the end of the school day, too long for children who are not mandated but have to bide their time before their after school programs start, and too short to be of any real use."

I know that for my son this is not a good choice. He is tired at the end of the day and he still has half an hour to an hour of homework to do when he gets home.

An Opportunity, Not a Punishment

Still, the poll results indicate that at least some students who are not required to attend the extra session will be taking advantage of the small-group tutoring. Thirty-five percent of poll respondents have a child mandated to attend the extra session, and 40 percent plan to have their child attend the extra session. "The idea of adding small group instruction to the school day is a good thing, and I think that if it is planned carefully and presented in a positive manner it will make a difference in students' achievement," as long as schools make an effort to prevent students who attend tutoring from being stigmatized, wrote parent Audrey Tindall. She adds that her child's school, Tompkins Square Middle School, has succeeded at presenting the extended day program as an opportunity, not a punishment.

Many parents said the idea of small group sessions is so good that the schools should aim to provide small group instruction for more students, and some of these parents are also upset that students not considered struggling will have their school day shortened by 10 minutes. "I do not think good students should be made to suffer by losing 50 minutes of instruction per week," wrote Ellen Reiser, a Manhattan East parent. Brooklyn parent Regina Poreda Ryan wrote that she felt "shortchanged" by the new schedule because "it seems that all children and families could benefit from an extended day. I was very surprised to learn that my child's school day would be shortened."

Several respondents commented that even if students might benefit academically from the extra time, they will be losing out on other needed activities, such as physical education, socialization and sleep. "While I vehemently agree that early intervention and small class size is extremely important, I know that for my son this is not a good choice," wrote Melissa McGill, whose son attends PS 39 in Brooklyn. "He is tired at the end of the day and he still has half an hour to an hour of homework to do when he gets home."

Devin, a student at Lehman High School, echoed this concern; when his middle school had an extended day program once a week, "I was tired from schoolwork and I did not learn anything!" he wrote.

A parent of a kindergarten student at the Children's School in Manhattan wrote, "I do not think that 5-year-olds need any more time sitting in school," adding that she will support the change only "if the school is able to integrate more phys. ed into the curriculum." Eugene Falik, a parent of a LaGuardia High School student agrees: "Children need more time to be children."

Ninety-two percent of the 300 respondents were parents, 6 percent were teachers and school officials and 2 percent were students. Roughly equal percentages came from the Bronx (21 percent), Brooklyn (27 percent), Manhattan (22 percent) and Queens (28 percent); 2 percent of respondents live on Staten Island. About 80 respondents provided free-response comments.

6

Year-Round Schooling Helps Struggling Students to Achieve

Joe Ann Barton

Joe Ann Barton is a former Rock Island elementary principal and director of curriculum and instruction/assistant superintendent at Scotia-Glenville Schools in New York State.

A changeover from a traditional school calendar to a year-round one has had a positive impact on the students and teachers at a school district in northwestern Illinois. For one thing, the emotional environment of the school changes when students and teachers have frequent breaks during the school year. There is less stress in the classroom and fewer episodes of absenteeism. But a mere change in the calendar without a fundamental change in instruction is meaningless. By implementing reforms in how teachers use their instruction time Rock Island school students, especially those from low-income families, have been able to show marked improvements in their district achievement tests and state assessments. The breaks in the school calendar (called intersessions) provide teachers with opportunities to further their professional development. Modified school calendars are not just for students who are academically behind; all students can benefit from the approach.

There is a stark change in the emotional environment of a school when you take charge of the clock. Two years ago, Thomas Jefferson Elementary School in Rock Island-Milan

Joe Ann Barton, "Taking Charge of Time: Why Year-Round Schooling Works for This Illinois District," *District Administration*, vol. 39, February 2003, p. 20. Copyright © 2003 Professional Media Group, LLC. Reproduced by permission.

(Ill.) School District #41 moved to a year-round calendar. On a recent Friday, Principal Rick Loy remarks, "I haven't had one student sent to the office all week. And I know why. We've just had two weeks off, everyone is refreshed, remotivated and their fire has been rekindled." Instead of hearing teachers and students asking when the next vacation is, Loy says they're just excited to be back.

"Having three months off in the summer isn't appropriate anymore, especially when you consider children who come to school who are already behind . . . because of their home environment or [undeveloped] language skills," says Darryl Taylor, principal of Grant Elementary School. "You know these children are going to have serious problems achieving, and the learning gap widens as they get older." With a year-round calendar, he says, "The kids feel less ground down, and the teachers feel more effective and energized."

Located in northwestern Illinois on the bluffs of the Mississippi River, Rock Island has switched all of its schools to a year-round calendar. With the traditional school calendar of nine months in session and three months off, Loy and Taylor note that students and teachers were showing significant signs of stress and fatigue by November; absenteeism and student discipline were more prevalent.

But with a year-round schedule, it's different. "We have many students who struggle to achieve academic success in school," says Superintendent David Markward. "We need to take advantage of every opportunity that we think is logical for them to be successful." A modified calendar, he says, has provided "educators [with] a time to step back—a time for teachers to make mid-course corrections before learning problems become achievement gaps."

How the Change to Year-Round Schooling Was Implemented

Two of Rock Island's elementary schools served as alternative calendar pilot sites, Horace Mann in 1991 and Grant Intensive

Basic in 1994. Horace Mann became a "choice" school, where students apply to attend and parents sign a contract to be supportive and active partners in their child's education. The school implemented multi-age classrooms, with teachers and students remaining together for three years. Grant Intensive piloted an extended calendar with 10 additional school days per year. Both schools have breaks for teachers and students at significant times.

The community felt [the modified schedule] offered the best of both worlds . . .

By 1999, the Board of Education began examining the pilots to decide whether they provided a better educational system and whether year-round calendars would make sense for the rest of the district, Markward says. Through informational meetings, he and the board explained to the individual school communities that it was up to each of them to decide about their calendar. Nationally, about 3,225 schools operate on a year-round schedule, according to the National Association of Year-Round Education.

The public's input was sought next. A district-wide committee created and distributed an informational survey, which sought input from parents, students, teachers and more than 35 local businesses.

Results were mailed directly to Augustana College, where they were tabulated for a report. Markward remembers those anxious moments when a professor came to see him with the results. "I held my breath because I had no idea . . . the results would show that an overwhelming majority of the community would agree to move forward with a calendar change."

The next step was to configure the right calendar. So the board held a series of community meetings. The decision: a modified calendar of nine weeks in session then two weeks off for each of the four quarters, culminating in an eight-week summer.

Markward says the community felt the schedule offered "the best of both worlds. . . . You can't change the history of our country. We know that summer is a pretty important thing. Oh, we can say that, gosh we should think education-ally about the use of summer time. But in the real world, there just are things that our society is built around and sum-mer is pretty important in the scheme of things."

Rock Island's year-round calendar adoption became a catalyst for implementing significant instructional changes.

Three months later, the Board of Education gave Mark-ward the okay to begin the 2001–2002 school year with a modified calendar for a five-year trial period with a yearly evaluation. Administrators at Horace Mann and Grant re-quested that they be allowed to keep their current calendars, as per their pilot status, an exception the board granted.

Changes in Instruction Lead to Better Student Outcomes

Without other changes, the act of altering a school's calendar proves insignificant. Rock Island's year-round calendar adop-tion became a catalyst for implementing significant instruc-tional changes. What takes place in the classroom is driven by the individual teacher's abilities, and new professional devel-opment opportunities have helped them become better teach-ers.

Markward says, "I just returned from the Francis Willard Elementary School where the poverty rate is 90 percent, but the student scores on the district achievement tests and state assessments are among the highest in the district. We think that happens because the teachers and administration work incredibly hard together." Also important to the district are creative cohesive principal-teacher relationships with a focus on student achievement.

Administrators in Rock Island see exceptional teaching as interactive—teachers engaging students actively in their learning. Quality teachers lead students to information by letting them discover answers, by helping them to develop critical thinking skills and to become problem solvers. Classroom teachers serve as resource providers and guides to student learning.

Teachers attend professional development sessions during a day or two during each of the two- or three-week breaks . . .

The district gives schools autonomy in planning professional development activities. At Horace Mann school, for example, one less teacher on staff provides money for in-depth professional development and classroom materials, says Principal Tom Berg.

Loy says the modified school calendar's intercessions are critical for professional development time. "You can't provide the professional development that is at the heart of getting good student achievement results unless teachers have quality, sustained professional development that is not done on top of their teaching load.

"After awhile, the quality . . . becomes diluted or doesn't have the desired impact on the classroom because the teacher rushed back to pick up where they left off," he adds.

Instead, at Thomas Jefferson, teachers attend professional development sessions during a day or two during each of the two- or three-week breaks, as well as a day or two over the longer summer break and at a few times throughout the school year. With this schedule, teachers have time for reflection, Loy says.

Taylor explains that Rock Island began its quest for better use of time when a community member brought an important document to the attention of the Board of Education. It was a 1994 National Education Commission report, "Prisoners of Time," which says learning becomes liberated when time is unlocked, or made an adjustable resource. Rock Island's teachers and students are more energized and actively engaged in classes because the district found a way to unlock the clock.

"Modified calendars are not just beneficial for children who are at-risk or children of poverty," says Taylor. "This is an approach to help all students because it gives everyone an opportunity to excel and to go beyond. We're looking for opportunities for all kids to do better."

7

Summer Vacation Is No Longer Necessary

Frederick M. Hess

Frederick M. Hess is a resident scholar and director of education policy studies at AEI.

The summer vacation is a remnant of an earlier, mainly agricultural America when children were needed to help their families work on farms. Those days are long gone, and the school year should reflect the realities of 21ˢᵗ-century family life and the demands of a changing economy. Low-income, minority children do not benefit from a three-month summer vacation and its accompanying learning loss. They are better off attending classes during the summer instead of wasting time at home or on the streets. Their parents would also be freed from the burden of finding suitable day-care or activities for them. There are many groups that want to retain the long summer break, however. These include some teacher unions and the summer activity industry such as amusement parks, summer camps, and resorts. The states should pass laws that restrict the permissible school year.

Can our kids afford to take summer vacation? Right now [July 2006], about 50 million children are on summer vacation across the United States. Many are discovering new interests at summer camp, playing ball at the Y, or traveling with Mom and Dad. But millions of others are loitering in parking lots and shopping malls, cruising iffy websites, and slouching

Frederick M. Hess, "Summer Vacation of Our Discontent," *www.washingtonpost.com*, July 12, 2006. Reproduced by permission of the author.

toward academic disaster. For this second group, it's time to take a fresh look at the traditional summer break.

Summer vacation once made good sense—back when we lived in a brawn-based economy, academic achievement mattered less, an absence of air conditioning or modern hygiene turned crowded schools into health risks, and children had moms who were home every day.

Historian Kenneth Gold has noted that summer vacation, as we know it, was an invention of the mid-19th-century belief that "too much schooling impaired a child's and a teacher's health." Community leaders fretted that summer was a "period of epidemics, and most fruitful of diseases generally," and sought to keep children at home or send them to the countryside.

In that era, the nation's first professional educators believed that too much schooling would exhaust both teacher and student. They thought that placid summers under parental supervision would be more beneficial than time spent in humid, crowded schools.

Summer vacation can be a massive inconvenience for today's middle-class families.

The Current Reality

Today, things have changed. We know that, for today's children, knowledge and academic skills will be critical to their future success and happiness. In many communities, children are safer in well-run schools than they are at home alone.

Other advanced nations don't provide an American-style summer vacation. Most industrialized nations offer no more than seven consecutive weeks of vacation. Meanwhile, American school districts offer up to thirteen.

In a long-gone world of plentiful manufacturing jobs and self-contained economies, such comparisons mattered less. Today, however, our children will find themselves competing with peers from Europe, India, and China for lucrative and rewarding brain-based jobs.

Summer vacation can also be a massive inconvenience for today's middle-class families. In the 1960s, reports the Population Resource Center, more than 60% of families consisted of a father working out of the house, a stay-at-home mother, and multiple children. Now, as U.S. Census data show, two-thirds of American children live in households where two parents work or with a single working parent, meaning no one is home to supervise children during the summer. For these families, summer vacation can be more an obstacle than a break. Parents must find ways to occupy their children's time and to monitor their socializing and web usage from work.

The nation's golf courses, amusement parks, and beachside resorts depend heavily on a cheap teen workforce.

The Urban Institute reports that, at most, just 30% of school-aged children in families with an employed primary caretaker are cared for by a parent during the summer. The Urban Institute study also notes that 41% of working families with school-age children pay for child care during the summer, typically spending about 8% of their summertime earnings. Meanwhile, expensive school facilities, computers, texts, and transportation sit idle.

Summer Vacation and Low-Income Kids

But the biggest problem with summer vacation today may be its impact on the academic achievement of low-income kids. In scores of studies, researchers—including scholars at places like the Johns Hopkins Center for Summer Learning and the Northwest Regional Educational Laboratory—have reported that these students lose significant academic ground in the summertime, while their more advantaged peers—those more likely to read and attend pricey summer camps—do not.

This has been a big factor in aggravating the "achievement gap" for urban and minority children. Programs with extended school years have had much success in boosting the achievement of these kids. The widely praised KIPP Academies, for instance, have employed a lengthened school year and a mandatory 3–4 week summer school session to boost achievement among their predominantly minority and urban students.

Today, "modified-calendar" schools exist in 46 states but enroll barely two million kids—about 5% of all K-12 students. Why aren't more schools offering an extended academic calendar?

One fierce opponent is the "summer activity industry." The nation's golf courses, amusement parks, and beachside resorts depend heavily on a cheap teen workforce. Movie theaters want teens with spending money, and the summer camp industry depends on families needing a place for their kids.

Additional schooling should not be an invitation to drudgery or an attack on childhood.

Teachers unions, too, are reluctant to see the school year extended. Efforts to add even two or three days to the academic year typically provoke objections from teachers and angry opposition from union officials.

What Should Be Done

Let's be clear: This is not a "national problem" or a uniform one. Summer vacations are still a wonderful time for many families and communities. Legislators need not pursue one-size-fits-all solutions to "fix" the school calendar.

Rather, it's time to acknowledge that 19th-century school practices may be a poor fit for many of today's families. It should be much easier for interested families to find schools that operate into or through the summer.

State officials should strike down laws—often supported by the summer recreation industry—that restrict the permissible school year for most schools. They should also help provide the operational funds necessary to support schools that operate through the summer.

School boards and superintendents should encourage more of their schools to move in this direction and appropriately compensate teachers and staff. Extending the school year will have the added benefit of helping to make teaching a full-time, more lucrative profession for educators who choose to work in these schools.

Additional schooling should not be an invitation to drudgery or an attack on childhood. It would allow schools to include more recess and athletics throughout the year, give teachers more time to conduct rich and imaginative lessons, and provide more time for music and the arts—all without compromising academic instruction.

Summer vacation can be a grand thing. But in the 21st century, for many children and families, it may also be an anachronism.

8

Summer Break Is Important to Students and Families

Joe Matthews

Joe Matthews is a staff writer for the Los Angeles Times.

Many urban school districts began to move to year-round calendars during the 1980s as a response to school overcrowding. Over 200 schools in the Los Angeles Unified School District now have a year-round calendar. Having students attend school year-round may not be a good thing, however. The nation's long summer break is not only a cherished American tradition but is necessary for the mental and physical well-being of the child. Some psychologists believe that too much study is detrimental to a child's mental health and children need time away from the regimentation of school. Scholars such as the education reformer Horace Mann argued on behalf of a long summer vacation. Mann wanted teachers to have time off to better prepare themselves in their chosen profession. The freedom from study and lack of schedules associated with summer vacation is good for students and their families and is good social policy too.

Ashley Sturgeon sat outside El Segundo High School on a hot August day, chatting with her sister and dreading the end of summer vacation.

Ashley and her sister Amber, who is starting seventh grade, have been told that the summer break is a tradition born in rural society.

But they see simpler reasons for the respite. "It's a good idea, whether you live in the city or on a farm," said Ashley, who will be in 11th grade. "Without the summer off, we might go insane."

The Sturgeons unwittingly have a better sense of the summer vacation's origins than most modern educators—or so suggests a book set to be published next year.

The book, "School's In: The History of Summer Education in American Public Schools," argues that the notion of summer vacation as an artifact of agrarian life is pure myth.

The history's author, City University of New York scholar Kenneth M. Gold, is running against a tide of public contentions to the contrary.

Summer vacation marked a conscious recognition of the value of rest . . .

The Value of Rest

In recent months, school superintendents in California, New Mexico, New York, Alabama and Arkansas have cited the vacation's rural origins in scrapping what they see as an outdated break and moving to year-round calendars.

Gov. Gray Davis and members of his administration made references to the vacation's supposed agrarian origins earlier this year when they proposed to shorten it for middle-school students. In writing about extended school years, dozens of newspapers—their writers far removed from the spring planting and fall harvest seasons of the farm—routinely perpetuate the theory. Earlier this year, the Los Angeles Times reported that the traditional calendar "is rooted in an agrarian lifestyle that has all but disappeared."

Gold argues, however, that summer vacation marked a conscious recognition of the value of rest, not a vestige of the farm labor cycle. As such, its misunderstood history holds lessons for modern educators in resolving questions that go beyond how to make use of July and August.

The 19th century Americans who created the modern school calendar were mostly city dwellers who wrestled with familiar issues, Gold contends. They wanted to increase attendance, prevent dropouts and provide as much schooling as possible—without breaking school budgets.

As a result, the first urban schools did not take the summer off, Gold writes. The charity system that was the forerunner of New York City's public schools operated year-round. By the 1840s, New York, Baltimore and Philadelphia all had about 11 months of school. In rural areas, school let out so students could work in the fields—but those breaks came in the spring and fall. School was in session in winter and summer.

What changed? Urbanization was one factor. City elites could afford to leave town for cooler climes. School officials, battling absenteeism, saw little advantage in opening schools on summer days or on holidays when many students wouldn't show up. Political pressures to standardize the school calendar across cities often led campuses to "the lowest common denominator"—in other words, less school.

A century of summer vacations has created a culture of summer . . .

Educational scholars also played their part. The influential 19th century psychiatrist Amariah Brigham, who closely studied children, wrote that too much schooling was contributing to a "growing tide of insanity" among the young. The poor quality of school buildings—and the heat of summer—fueled concerns about the physical health of students. Horace Mann was among those reformers who wanted to professionalize teaching. He saw the summer vacation as a good time for professional development that would further that goal.

By the turn of the century, the reformers had won. With a few exceptions, Gold writes, a September-to-June school year was the standard.

The Move to Year-Round Schedule vs. a Culture of Summer

So standard that the summer break's origins were forgotten when urban crowding caused districts to begin moving to year-round schedules in the 1980s. By 1992, more than 1 million American kids were in year-round public schools. In the Los Angeles Unified School District, 224 schools now have the year-round calendar.

The theory of the summer break's agrarian origins has proved to be a handy argument: We're not adding school— we're reversing an anachronism.

That is how the Paramount Unified School District, for instance, explains its switch a few years back to year-round elementary and middle schools. "The traditional calendar was instituted decades and decades ago when it was a more agrarian society," Supt. Jay Wilbur said. "People needed summer breaks to work in the fields. We don't need that now."

Gold is a historian of education, not a theorist, but he wonders about the effect of the year-round changes. A century of summer vacations has created a culture of summer, of freedom and romance and personal growth held deeply from New York to El Segundo. That culture may be worth preserving.

"Increasing summer school may be a good educational policy for raising standardized test scores," he writes, "but is it good social policy to tamper with the season during which many families and friends forge their most enduring bonds and memories?"

Just ask the students. Without summer, they might go insane.

9

Schools on a Balanced Calendar Make Better Use of Time

Joan Hamilton, Sheryl Johnston, Jane Marshall, and Carolyn Shields

Joan Hamilton is the Principal of Roberta Bondar Public School; Sheryl Johnston is a 3rd grade teacher at Roberta Bondar Public School; Jane Marshall is Acting Vice Principal of Roberta Bondar Public School; and Carolyn Shields is Head of Educational Organization and Leadership at the University of Illinois at Urbana-Champaign.

Roberta Bondar Public School, a K–8 public school in a suburb of Toronto, Ontario challenges the status quo of how U.S. and Canadian schools use time. Most of the 1,100 students come from first-generation immigrant families. Many speak English as their second language. Roberta Bondar runs on a balanced, year-round calendar. Instead of a long summer vacation, students have holidays that are spread out over the school year. Instead of a long lunch break, students enjoy two, 45-minute recesses. Intersessions are offered during each vacation break and enable the school to provide remedial and enrichment classes. The classes are optional and are offered at a price families can afford. Teacher motivation at Roberta Bondar is high: teachers want to give students the extra help they need, and they get paid a higher salary for their time. In addition, teachers are continually giving feedback to the administration in order to better customize instruction for the student population. In this way the school can target areas where students need help and bridge the gaps in learning.

A long summer vacation in which students forget much of what they have learned is far from ideal for learning. At Roberta Bondar Public School, which serves K–8 students in a Toronto, Ontario, suburb, we follow what we call the balanced calendar model—essentially, year-round schooling. This schedule frees us to provide priceless instructional time and enrichment to our 1,100 students, most of whom come from first-generation immigrant families.

The balanced calendar model ... puts time on the side of students.

A Model of a Balanced Calendar

Roberta Bondar is one of a handful of Canadian schools using a balanced calendar. The model generally includes an alternative school year, a modified school day, and enhanced learning opportunities during breaks. Our students do have school holidays, but these holidays are distributed throughout the year. School starts in early August, five weeks before the traditional start date of early September. The five holiday weeks gained by starting in August are spread out; we have a two-week break in October, a three-week winter break, a week in February and a two-week spring break in March. Staff members and students also enjoy the month of July off.

Beyond reducing the summer learning loss, we strive to use the time that our students spend in school in the most efficient way for learning. We have modified our school day so that two 45-minute nutrition breaks replace the traditional lunch hour and two recesses. Because students spend less time transitioning between classes, they gain instructional time. We estimate that the balanced calendar model adds four to six weeks of instructional time to the school year.

During each break, we offer an intersession—optional remedial and enrichment classes at an affordable price. Intersessions provide students who need additional help with extra time for learning or a chance to learn through unconventional methods. Classes include a wide range of learning opportunities, from robotics to math to cooperative games.

Teachers Are Paid for Intersessions

Roberta Bondar's teachers eagerly signed up to teach our first intersession period last fall. Although teachers were paid additional salary for teaching during these periods, the chance to help students was as strong a motivator for our teachers as the higher pay. Before the classes began, we gathered feedback from classroom teachers to design learning opportunities that met the specific needs of the student group registered for intersession. For example, in creating a remedial reading class to support struggling readers in 1st and 2nd grade, we asked teachers to provide reading assessment data, to spell out their students' areas of greatest need, and to fill out learning profiles of their students, noting which students spoke English as a second language or had disability issues. Our goal, especially early in the year, was to focus instruction to close a specific learning gap.

Canadian and U.S. schools need new strategies related to scheduling time. A U.S. government report from the National Education Commission on Time and Learning concluded that,

> For the past 150 years, American schools have held time constant and let learning vary. The rule, only rarely voiced, is simple: Learn what you can in the time we make available. [Some] bright, hardworking students do reasonably well. Everyone else—from the typical student to the dropout—runs into trouble.

The balanced calendar model challenges the status quo of an outdated agrarian "school year" and maximizes the time students spend engaged in learning. The arrangement minimizes summer learning loss and offers remediation to struggling students while shattering the boredom of summer. It puts time on the side of students.

10

Extending the School Calendar Is a Last Recourse for Low-Performing Schools

V. Dion Haynes

V. Dion Haynes is a staff writer for the Washington Post.

Approximately 2.5 million students in about 3,000 public schools spread across the nation attend year-round schools. Some of these schools are in fast-growing school districts where administrators must find ways to accommodate rising student enrollments. Other public schools switch from traditional schedules to a year-round calendar as a way to reverse low-performance. These schools are often located in under-resourced urban settings with low-income, minority populations. In Washington, D.C., School Superintendent Clifford Janey proposes moving five low-performing schools to year-round calendars. For many school superintendents in districts like Washington, D.C. there are few options left. The current federal No Child Left Behind law allows students in low-performing schools to transfer to other, higher-achieving schools or to charter schools. However, in Washington there are not enough of these kinds of schools available for students to transfer to. The only solution is to try to reconfigure the school calendar for the low-performing schools and hope that student achievement levels rise as a result.

D.C. School Superintendent Clifford B. Janey is proposing year-round classes at five mainly low-achieving schools in an effort to give students more time in the classroom by shortening the long summer break.

The proposal, which is the school system's first attempt to adjust the traditional calendar, will probably ignite a local and nationwide debate: Education experts extol the benefits of a year-round calendar, citing studies that show significant knowledge loss over the summer, but many parents argue that children need downtime.

Janey said he expects to select the five schools—at least three of which would be low-performing—by December.

Charter schools . . . have drawn nearly 20,000 D.C. students in the past decade.

Running Out of Options

Janey has proposed adding as many as 20 days to the 180-day calendar at the five schools, in part because he says he is running out of options to help students in low-performing schools.

School system officials have said they will release data this month showing that a large number of District schools failed to meet academic benchmarks on a more rigorous student assessment introduced in the spring. Results will be worse than last year, officials said, when about 80 of 147 schools failed to reach academic goals under the previous exam.

The federal No Child Left Behind law gives students in low-performing schools the right to transfer to higher-achieving schools, but some say there will not be enough high-performing schools to accommodate the possible transfers.

"You can't talk about transferring anyone in this environment. You've got to take a radical approach" to boosting student achievement, said Carolyn N. Graham, the vice president of the Board of Education.

"The board is fully supportive of an aggressive approach," she said. Extra money to run the schools year-round, she said, would come from $8 million in annual savings from the board's decision in June to close five under-enrolled schools.

But Cherita Whiting, who is on the board of directors of the citywide PTA, said extending the school year into the summer would rob students of time with their families and at summer camp.

"Students need parent time, and they need time to themselves," said Whiting, who has a son at McKinley Technology High School in Eckington. "The administration needs to make sure the schools are doing what they're supposed to be doing from August to June" so that the year won't have to be extended.

Locally, only a few schools—including Samuel W. Tucker and Mount Vernon elementary schools in Alexandria and E.L. Haynes Public Charter School in Northwest Washington—are operating on a year-round or modified calendar. Rushern L. Baker III (D), a former state delegate, has called for year-round schooling in Prince George's County, where he is trying to unseat County Executive Jack B. Johnson (D) in the Sept. 12 primary.

The research on these things is mixed. We've got places where moving to year-round didn't affect performance.

Competing With Charter Schools

Janey's proposal is part of an effort to compete more aggressively with charter schools, which have drawn nearly 20,000 D.C. students in the past decade.

Most schools maintain the traditional 180-day calendar, instructing students in three-month blocks broken up by one to two months off.

In lengthening the academic year by about four weeks, the schools would maintain a calendar similar to the one used by the Knowledge Is Power Program, which runs a network of free open-enrollment, college-preparatory public schools in under-resourced communities nationwide, including two high-performing public charter schools and an upstart campus in the District.

The additional time, Janey said, would be used for tutoring and enrichment, including art and music classes and trips to museums.

Migration to the year-round schedule experienced its greatest boom in the 1990s, but has lost ground in recent years. The number of year-round schools nationwide dropped from 3,181 in 2003 to 2,850 this year, according to the National Association for Year-Round Education.

"The research on these things is mixed. We've got places where moving to year-round didn't affect performance," said Michael Casserly, executive director of the District-based Council of the Great City Schools, an advocacy organization representing the nation's largest urban public school districts.

But adding days to the school year "is likely to help," Casserly said.

Janey said he would ask officials from schools interested in switching to the year-round calendar to submit proposals. He also is negotiating with the Washington Teachers' Union to add a provision to an upcoming contract that would allow teachers to participate in the longer schedules.

Union President George Parker said he supports the concept. "The WTU is not opposed to looking at reasonable, research-based options that would make our schools better," he said.

11

Teachers Have Greater Job Satisfaction in Year-Round Schools

Shelly Gismondi Haser and Ilham Nasser

Shelly Gismondi Haser is an associate professor in the School of Education and Human Services at Marymount University and the program coordinator for the Marymount University/Fairfax County Professional Development Schools Partnership Program. Ilham Nasser has been a teacher and teacher trainer and counselor. She is a visiting researcher at the Center for Global Peace at American University.

Many schools that switch from a traditional school calendar to a year-round or modified school calendar do so because teachers are dissatisfied. Making the transition from a traditional school calendar to a year-round calendar is not without challenges, however. Teachers in several schools in Fairfax County, Virginia studied year-round schools before switching over. They worked with principals and the community to implement the changeover. Once teachers experience the year-round schedule and the opportunities intersessions provide for professional development or rejuvenation they are more content with their jobs, are more motivated, have a stronger commitment to their students, and are absent less from the classroom.

Green Meadow Elementary School (pseudonym) was built in 1955 and was recently renovated. Over the past forty-seven years, the school has grown to serve a diverse community. This Title I school had a student population comprised from over sixty countries with a recent enrollment of 572 students. The school was Fairfax County's first school to operate on a year-round or modified calendar.

Students at the school enjoyed the benefits of a renovated building, which included a large library, larger classrooms, and a more aesthetically pleasing environment. Also, a wireless mobile computer lab afforded the opportunity to learn through cutting-edge technology practices. As expressed on the school's 2004 website, staff and community members believed that six principles guided their actions as professionals:

> All children can and will learn. Ethnicity, cultural and religious backgrounds, family education, income level, or conditions in the home do not affect the ability of the child to learn; nor will such factors decrease the exemplary effort given in teaching the students. Parents want and deserve the best education for their children and they deserve full support in coeducating their child or children.

Lack of Time Frustrated Teachers

This [viewpoint] is focused on the process by which this school switched from a traditional to a modified calendar, the principals' leadership styles as part of that process, and the resultant effect on teacher motivation under the new modified calendar. Green Meadow teachers were feeling frustrated in the mid-1990s by their lack of time for planning and reflection; they were truly interested in changing the instructional format of the school day and year in order to benefit the predominately minority, at-risk students at this school. The major frustration they voiced was the lack of sufficient instructional time to meet the needs of their students. So the teachers embarked on a plan for change. By 1998, the teachers had successfully spearheaded a three-year transition from the traditional calendar to a modified-calendar school through the support and guidance of the school and county administrators.

The whole idea to examine a year-round or modified calendar . . . actually came from a group of Green Meadow teachers—it was their initial idea!

This was the first year-round or modified-calendar school in the county, and it eventually paved the way for six other county elementary schools with similar student populations to move to a modified calendar.

Green Meadow had been functioning on a modified calendar for three years when the work for this case study started. During the interviews . . . teachers and specialists reflected and talked in great length about the transition process from a traditional calendar to a year-round or modified-calendar school, and the impact of the new calendar, which they felt enhanced the quality of their teaching or "job performance" and motivated them to want to teach in this high-needs school. Part of the former and current school administrators' discussions included their roles in the transition and post-transition years.

The following themes emerged from the discussions and observations at Green Meadow:

1. Teachers felt empowered through ownership of the transition process from a traditional to a modified-calendar school.

2. Teachers felt supported by their colleagues, school administrators, and county administrators for their work in changing to a modified calendar and in their teaching endeavors after the switch.

3. The calendar assisted in reducing professional stress and burnout and presented teachers with professional options not necessarily available in traditional calendar schools.

4. The school administrator's leadership style was a key factor in the teachers' motivation before, during, and after the transition from a traditional to a modified calendar school.

5. The alternative calendar presented a few obstacles.

The Idea Began With Teachers

The uniqueness of the transition in this school stems from the fact that teachers felt they had ownership over the process from a traditional to a year-round or modified-calendar school. This ownership seemed to play an important role in motivating teachers. In a preceding discussion, support from colleagues and superiors was cited as a factor for greater teacher motivation. Support alone and in and of itself may not be sufficient to motivate teachers without the empowerment that teachers said they needed. One of the best examples is that the whole idea to examine a year-round or modified calendar as a new school schedule actually came from a group of Green Meadow teachers—it was their initial idea!

Eighty-seven percent of the school community voted in favor of the idea, which was a great success for the teachers.

Green Meadow teachers took the lead in learning about year-round or modified-calendar schooling. They exerted much effort in attending conferences, visiting other schools, and gathering information about the model. Eventually the *teachers* came to the conclusion that this schedule was best for the majority of students. The teachers viewed themselves as an integral part of the decision-making process and implementation.

One teacher commented, "Our student body [has] mostly working parents with more than two jobs and they work all week. Not only does it [the calendar] give the children more time in school [via the intersessions] . . . they are in school rather than on the streets or just sitting in front of a television."

The previous principal who facilitated the teachers in the process noted that "The teachers had a common problem of how to teach such a large curriculum in just 180 days. They usually managed somehow but always complained about the fact that they don't have enough time. This was the beginning of a three-year self-examination process where *teachers* looked at the transition as a good possibility."

The Process

At the very beginning of the whole process, the principal told the teachers who complained about curriculum fragmentation due to scheduling: "Lets form a committee. . . . I am willing to hear your suggestions on how to deal with that." Eighteen enthusiastic teachers jumped at the opportunity. According to the teachers who took part in the transition, many of whom were veteran teachers, they formed a think tank open to all teachers. Members of the think tank brought ideas on how to increase learning time in a student-centered environment. In addition to a modified calendar, they also explored lengthening the school day or offering more summer school courses.

One of the teachers noticed an invitation to a conference on year-round education and brought the idea up at a meeting. Shortly thereafter, two teachers traveled to the conference to learn more about the idea and to check whether it might be a good model for their school. The teachers were excited about the information presented at the conference and shared the knowledge gained with the think tank. The group then decided to pursue changing from a traditional calendar into a year-round or modified-calendar school.

The succeeding principal, who had served as one of the teachers on the think tank committee, recalled: "There was a general excitement that this might be a solution to have more instructional time on hand but there was also skepticism that the county would not allow us to do so because of the cost and conflicting schedules."

Despite frustrations experienced at some junctures during the first years of the process, the committee kept studying the proposal while the [former] principal was communicating the teachers' findings to county administrators.

In the second year when teachers were convinced that they wanted to move on with the transition, they solicited input from the community. The principal immediately formed a steering committee made up of interested parents. The principal even took two parents and three more teachers to the next year-round education annual conference to learn more about intersessions and the whole idea of extended learning time. Meanwhile, teachers led community meetings. . . . According to the assistant principal, 87 percent of the school community voted in favor of the idea, which was a great success for the teachers. . . .

The school principal and assistant principal listened to concerns and worked toward win-win solutions.

The teachers revealed that they were all ready to transition to the new calendar by the end of the second year, but school board members and the superintendent, Dr. Daniel Domenech, requested that they wait a third year in order to work out all the details. The third year of preparation proved to be worthwhile as the principal and assistant principal worked out many details and logistics with the county, such as transportation, food services, and special education services.

The Teachers Were Supported in Many Ways

There were three levels of support that teachers felt were important to their efforts as they moved towards a year-round or modified calendar. Those levels were: the support from the county, the support from the school administration, and lastly, the support of fellow school colleagues who all shared the school's vision and mission revolving around the students and the modified calendar. The authors opine that each of those sources of support motivated teachers in their jobs, especially during the transition period.

The support the teachers received started at a higher level within the school system's hierarchy, specifically with their area director or "cluster director." The cluster director's responsibility was to oversee the principals and academic progress of the schools in a specific part of the county. The cluster director's support provided teachers with professional respect and confidence in pursuing the modified calendar option. Teachers articulated that the county-level administrators listened to their ideas and concerns through a small group of teacher representatives and school administrators) and worked with them, the teachers.

Teachers knew they had the option to look into a change in the instructional format in their school, which would include more time in school for students. At the beginning of the process, one teacher described how several teachers examined a handful of instructional models that allowed more learning time with children.

She said, "A few teachers read about year-round education and became interested in learning more about it. They went to the principal and asked her if they could attend a conference. The principal approved the idea and covered the cost of it." . . .

The cluster director helped to obtain the school board's approval of the transition as a whole. The transition required additional budgets: in this case it was about $250,000 in additional cost for staffing, transportation, and intersessions. This was costly, but the county was willing to invest in the school. In addition to cost, the cluster director also assisted in working out many details and schedules relating to food services, custodians, office staff, staffing intersessions, and special education services, etc. Without the support of the county, those important details would not have been worked out as smoothly, or possibly at all, as the previous principal recounted in her interview.

The cluster director and other higher-level county administrators played an important role in securing the county school board's approval to expand the services of additional professionals at Green Meadow once it changed to a modified calendar. Those resources and services included a psychologist, social worker, resource teachers, and a parent liaison (Spanish speaking), who helped communicate with and meet the needs of the diverse community that was predominately Hispanic.

Transitioning to a different school calendar was a major change, and without the leadership of the school administration through their cooperative approach, teachers would have most likely resented the idea and fought it. At Green Meadow, many teachers stated that the school principal and assistant principal listened to concerns and worked toward win-win solutions. These interactions helped to develop a trusting relationship between teachers and school administrators. One teacher mentioned: "Our principal lets us do our job, and we have ownership in teaching the students."

Teachers viewed the new schedule as an improvement in their work conditions, since they had frequent two-week breaks throughout twelve months.

A Cooperative Approach

Another example given by teachers to illustrate the cooperative approach taken by the school administration was that breaks or intersession time was structured to allow teachers to plan for the following quarter. Actually, this was a secondary reason behind transitioning to a modified calendar according to the school principal who said: "The idea [for a modified-calendar school] was also to give teachers more think time. If teachers in a specific grade level agree to meet together for a block of time during intersessions, they received a stipend for curriculum planning and reflection."

In fact, concurring sentiments were expressed by several teachers who cited a need to sometimes "step back" from the classroom, which usually happens just around the intersession or school quarter breaks. One teacher put it this way: "I have time during intersessions to just reflect about rearranging my classroom and tweaking classroom management. I come in and do all of this and get paid for it."

One teacher described the shared vision with the principal and assistant principal as "the number-one interest is children and children being successful." A veteran teacher stated, "I really like the way teachers and teams collaborate. They seem to have a vision and a goal and to know their kids and what they need. Kids come first, definitely."

In fact, all of the teachers who were interviewed expressed their agreement on the statement that their school serves children first and that the principal and assistant principal played an important role in spreading that vision among the staff and students. The administrators were described as role models for their teachers. . . .

The Role of Intersessions in Job Satisfaction

Most teachers at schools that operate on traditional calendars feel they have few professional options. However, many Green Meadow teachers had previously worked in schools that operated under the traditional calendar and were thereby able to compare that system with the year-round or modified calendar. Many Green Meadow teachers commented that the intersessions created more professional choices and flexibility, which increased their satisfaction in their chosen profession.

Teachers viewed the new schedule as an improvement in their work conditions, since they had frequent two-week breaks throughout twelve months. These scheduled breaks seemed to decrease teachers' feelings of professional stress and burnout. The assistant principal noted that the school data on teacher absenteeism showed that that had decreased on the modified calendar, which meant fewer substitute teachers were needed, and therefore, less money was spent. Also, the option of instructing an intersession class provided Green Meadow teachers with several professional choices that in turn dramatically enhanced their motivation or drive to continue to teach.

Professionally, the intersessions provided four primary options for teachers, which were:

- A change from teaching the same academic subject(s) and/or the same grade level

- An opportunity to earn extra money

- Additional professional reflection and curriculum planning time

- Nontraditional periodic breaks or vacation time away from the school

Green Meadow teachers who chose to teach during the intersessions did so because they enjoyed working with other students from different grades, or they liked teaching other subjects or hobbies, and last but not least, they liked earning extra pay. Even though many intersession classes focused on remediation or academics under the county curriculum, there were curriculum extension or enrichment classes offered as well. For example, several teachers who were fluent in a foreign language used the intersession time to teach children Spanish or Chinese. Some teachers taught cooking classes, geography, and visual arts. Others focused on technology and physical education. All of the intersession classes were based on the county's Program of Study (POS) and the Virginia Standards of Learning (SOL). Each intersession class had a unit outline, lesson plans, and assessments.

The opportunity to teach during intersessions gave Green Meadow teachers on maternity or family leave a chance to keep their hand in the profession. As the assistant principal stated: "We always try something once ... we try to be flexible. There were two teachers on maternity leave who were interested in teaching during the intersession, and arrangements were made for them to share an intersession class and keep in the [teaching] loop."

Numerous teachers continually chose to teach an intersession class and earn extra money, but those who chose not to work during the intersessions cited the opportunity to relax and rejuvenate away from school. Teachers took advantage of the nontraditional breaks by taking a cruise in October or a long ski holiday in January, both of which were not feasible under a traditional school calendar. One teacher said: "On this [modified] calendar I can take my mom to Italy in October, something I've never been able to do before." ...

The fact that both teachers and students have breaks from each other may be one reason for the more relaxed and productive school environment.

The break during intersession also provided those teachers who had decided not to teach an opportunity to read professional journals or books and to attend workshops and conferences. One teacher mentioned the fact that she had the time to "catch up on professional reading or even attend some professional development workshops."

Several teachers talked about using the break or intersession time for planning—an advantage that was provided every nine weeks through the modified-calendar schedule. This was not usually possible when Green Meadow was functioning on a traditional school calendar. Other teachers as mentioned earlier in the chapter, took advantage of the opportunity to teach other grade levels or to come into school during the intersession break to plan for the next quarter, for which they were paid.

The school administrators hoped that all of those professional options and opportunities offered by the modified calendar would keep the teachers refreshed, stimulated, and excited about teaching.

A Decrease in Stress for Teachers Helps All

Teachers on a traditional calendar feel stressed and get burned out more quickly during the lengthy traditional school year. This trend has been especially noticed in Title I schools, where teachers work with diverse children in quite demanding environments. At Green Meadow, there was a significant discussion by teachers on the decrease in professional stress because of the available breaks staggered throughout twelve months. One teacher commented:

> On the traditional calendar, I was wiped out by April. To do a good job as a teacher [in a high-needs school] took a lot out of me; I even thought of early retirement. Now, on the year-round education cycle, I get systematic breaks, the kids get breaks from me, and we're ready to work together again.

In fact, the school administration noticed that this model decreased teacher absenteeism. The assistant principal explained:

> Because they [teachers] get frequent breaks, teachers don't need to take off as many mental health days. Also teachers try to schedule their doctor's appointments during intersessions, so they don't have to take leave, which comes back around to the kids' benefit. If teachers take fewer days off, they're in the classroom more, and more learning is most likely going on than with a substitute.

The assistant principal explained that this model played an important role in reducing teachers' stress levels because it also reduced children's feelings of stress as well. The school had less discipline referrals or problems because of these schedule. . . .

The fact that both teachers and children have breaks from each other may be one reason for the more relaxed and productive school environment.

Stress and burnout are major reasons why teachers leave the profession. But at Green Meadow, teacher retention was found to be very high. Few teachers left the school unless they had newborns or had to relocate because of their spouse's job. At a time when many high-needs schools in the Washington, D.C., metropolitan area experienced shortages and fewer teaching applicants, the principal displayed a stack of applications from teachers interested in employment at the school.

12

Multi-Tracking Is Not for Everyone

Glori Chaika

Glori Chaika teaches English at Slidell Junior High School in Slidell, Louisiana and is a frequent contributor to Education World.

School districts operating on a year-round calendar choose one of two schedules: a single-track schedule in which all students are on vacation at the same time or a multi-track schedule in which a percentage of students are on vacation at a given time. Multi-tracking allows school districts to get the most use out of their school facilities and thus save money. It also helps keep down the size of classes in districts with large student enrollments. Multi-tracking has serious drawbacks, however. Maintaining the schools is a problem because they are in continual use. Teachers and students on vacation have to move their belongings to make room for incoming teachers and students. Scheduling events such as open houses and state tests has to be done twice. Multi-tracking is also tough for parents with several children in the school district when each child is on a different track. Even students who live in the same neighborhood can be on different schedules.

Do year-round schools enhance student learning, or are they a costly, hectic, and largely ineffective cure for the nation's educational ills? Those involved in year-round schools—school superintendents, specialists, researchers, teachers, and principals—share their views with Education World readers.

"At a time when the public is actually demanding greater retention of information and higher levels of achievement from the nation's students, educators and parents must change business as usual and challenge the wisdom of maintaining that long summer of forgetting," Dr. Charles Ballinger, executive director of the National Association for Year-Round Education, told Education World.

More than 2 million students in close to 3,000 public schools in 41 states and 610 school districts attend year-round schools. As quickly as schools—especially those in fast-growing districts—adopt year-round schooling, others, stating that hot classrooms outweigh the possible educational plusses, revert to traditional schedules.

Tracking Students: Single or Multi Schedules

"Year-round schooling" is actually a misnomer. Students in year-round schools do not stay in school all year. In most cases, they are in school the same number of days as students on traditional calendars. Instead of a three-month vacation, schedules include several shorter vacations, or intercessions, spaced throughout the year.

Because the classrooms were always used, maintenance was affected.

Year-round schools operate on a single-track schedule—all students are on vacation at the same time—or a multi-track schedule—a percentage of students are on vacation at a given time. Students can opt to spend time with their families or take advantage of remedial or enrichment programs during their intercessions.

Saving Money Through Multitracking

Multi-tracking allows schools to enroll more students than buildings would ordinarily hold. The money saved through multi-tracking can be considerable. Florida's Marion County system estimates a savings of more than $12 million in construction costs because the district switched to multi-track year-round schooling. California's Oxnard School District estimates savings of approximately $20 million. Tom Payne, year-round education consultant for the California Department of Education, told *Education World* he estimates the state of California saved more than $4 billion when it switched 1027 of the 1517 single-track year-round schools to multi-track schedules.

In addition to increasing school-building capacity, reducing class size, and maximizing use of facilities, advocates of multi-track year-round scheduling say it

- reduces teacher burnout, student stress, drop-out rates, and discipline problems;

- increases student retention and achievement;

- decreases the amount of school vandalism and the number of burglaries;

- allows families to take vacations at times that are more advantageous, avoiding crowds and inflated rates.

Teachers might be on one track while their own children were on another track ...

A Hectic Life For All

In some districts, because of increased administration, utility, maintenance, and/or transportation costs, predicted savings have not materialized. Life can also be hectic on a multi-track year-round schedule.

"Because multi-track schools try to keep rooms at 100 percent capacity, it means a lot of moving," Becky Hitt, a special education teacher at Imperial Beach (California) Elementary School, told *Education World*. "In my previous school, before intercessions, my students and I needed to put all our belongings into wheeled cabinets that were then stored in a shed until we came back. A 'roving' teacher went into my room while we were away. Students and teachers who roved never had a room of their own. Every four weeks or so, they packed all their belongings into wheeled cabinets and wheeled them into the next available room. Every time we came back from our break, we needed to set up again.

"Because the classrooms were always used, maintenance was affected," added Hitt. "That school was dirty. Maintenance people work when it fits their schedule, whether or not it disrupts the classroom. I remember walking into my room one day to find my carpets clean but wet, an incredible odor in my room, my desks everywhere, my bulletin boards curled from the moisture.

"It was especially tough," she noted, "when I was on a track that ended in August, and the new school year began just a few days later. If a teacher taught a new subject or a new grade level, there was no time to prepare."

Richard Vale, a seventh-grade math teacher at James Rutter Middle School in Sacramento, California, sees some other drawbacks. Vale told *Education World*: "Almost everything had to be done twice: open house, school pictures, state testing, everything—someone was always off track when one of those events was scheduled. All band members at our school, like all athletes, had to be on the same track. They might have been on a different track from the other kids in their neighborhood or even other members of their family.

"Then there's the heat here," Vale continued. "In the summertime, we switch to an earlier schedule. School starts at about 6:50 a.m. or so, and ends around 1:10. We do this even though our school is air-conditioned because kids can't participate in PE at 3:00 in the afternoon when it's 110 degrees!"

Sixth-grade teacher Charlotte Griswold told *Education World* that it was possible for parents at her school—Oak Hill Middle School in Clear Lake, California—to have children on three different schedules. Teachers might be on one track while their own children were on another track or attended traditional schools.

In some other places, the elementary school is on a year-round schedule, but the middle and high schools are on traditional schedules. When high school students aren't off at the same time their younger siblings are, scheduling day care becomes a nightmare for some parents.

"Multi-track year-round schedules can be difficult," acknowledged Leroy Small, an educator for more than 30 years and now a consultant for the California Department of Education's Year-Round Education Advisory Committee.

Teacher Becky Hitt couldn't agree more. "When I found an opening in a single-track school, I jumped at it," she told *Education World*.

Organizations to Contact

The editors have compiled the following list of organizations concerned with the issues debated in this book. The descriptions are derived from materials provided by the organizations. All have publications or information available for interested readers. The list was compiled on the date of publication of the present volume; the information provided here may change. Be aware that many organizations take several weeks or longer to respond to inquiries, so allow as much time as possible.

The American Enterprise Institute
1150 Seventeenth Street, N.W., Washington, DC   20036
(202) 862-5800 • fax: (202) 862-7177
Web site: www.aei.org

The American Enterprise Institute for Public Policy Research is a private, not-for-profit institution dedicated to research and education on various issues such as government, politics, economics, and education. The AEI was founded in 1943 and sponsors research and conferences and publishes books, monographs, and periodicals. Its Web site posts its publications and transcripts of its conferences.

American Federation of Teachers (AFT)
555 New Jersey Avenue, NW, Washington, DC   20001
(202) 879-4400
Web site: www.aft.org

The American Federation of Teachers is a teacher's union organized to improve the lives of teachers and their families, address issues of importance to teachers, and improve the services they provide to their communities. The AFT publishes reports, lobbies for legislation of importance to the teaching profession, and tracks issues in education.

Center for American Progress
1333 H Street, N.W., Washington, DC   20005
(202) 682-1611
Web site: www.americanprogress.org

The Center for American Progress is a progressive think tank dedicated to improving the lives of Americans through ideas and action. The scholars and fellows at the center explore innovative solutions to the nation's problems and present them to legislators and others for debate.

Center for Education Reform
1001 Connecticut Avenue, N.W., Washington, DC   20036
(202) 822-9000 • fax: (202) 822-5077
Web site: www.edreform.com

The Center for Education Reform advocates on behalf of improving education and schools for all children. CER calls for reforms that produce high standards, accountability, and freedom, such as strong charter school laws, school choice programs for children most in need, common sense teacher initiatives, and proven instructional programs. Its Web site includes information on issues such as school choice, rates charter schools, and tracks the latest changes in the states with regard to school calendars and curriculum.

Massachusetts 2020
One Beacon Street, Boston, MA   02108
(617) 724-6747 • fax: (617) 723-6746
Web site: www.mass2020.org

Massachusetts 2020 was founded in 2000 with the goal of expanding after-school and summer learning opportunities for children across the state. The agenda for 2007 and beyond includes an increased focus on rethinking time and learning within the traditional school system. Massachusetts 2020 has been a lead partner in launching several major initiatives including Boston's After-School for All Partnership, the largest public-private partnership (over $26 million) dedicated to children in Boston's history. Massachusetts 2020 has worked in partnership with the Massachusetts Department of Education to oversee and assist the conversion of a number of schools to a school schedule that is 30 percent longer than the traditional school schedule.

The National Association for Year-Round Education
6401 Linda Vista Road, Room 412
San Diego, California 92111
(619) 276-5296 • fax: (619) 571-5754
Web site: www.NAYRE.org

The National Association for Year-Round Education (NAYRE) is a clearinghouse for information on year-round education and the subject of time and learning. Year-round education reorganizes the traditional school calendar to shorten the three-month summer vacation and allow for shorter breaks spread throughout the school year. NAYRE's Web site contains statistics, research abstracts, calendars, and a history of the issue of year-round schooling.

National Education Association (NEA)
1201 16th Street, NW, Washington, DC 20036-3290
(202) 833-4000 • fax: (202) 822-7974
Web site: www.nea.org

The National Education Association is the nation's largest professional employee organization with more than 3 million members. The association's goal is to work for the advancement of public education from the pre-school level to college and beyond. The NEA has affiliates at the state and local levels.

Summer Matters!!
16 Hopson Road, Jacksonville Beach, Florida 32250
(904) 249-2468
Web site: www.summermatters.com

Summer Matters!! is the main Web-based network for supporters of the traditional school calendar. The information contained includes recent research, media accounts, and data from grassroots organizations. The information is compiled by Billee Bussard, a former journalist and editorial writer for the *Florida Times-Union* in Jacksonville.

Bibliography

Books

David Elkind — *The Power of Play: How Spontaneous, Imaginative Activities Lead to Happier, Healthier Children.* New York: De Capo Lifelong Press, 2007.

Patricia Gandara — *The Dimensions of Time and the Challenge of School Reform.* Albany NY: SUNY Press, 2000.

K.M. Gold — *School's In: The History of Summer Education in American Public Schools.* New York: Peter Lang.

Sarah H. Huyvaert — *Time Is of the Essence: Learning in Schools.* Boston: Allyn & Bacon, 1998.

Etta Kralovec — *Schools That Do Too Much: Wasting Time and Money in Schools and What We Can All Do About It.* Boston: Beacon Press, 2003.

Carolyn Shields and Steven Lynn Oberg — *Year-Round Schooling: Promises and Pitfalls.* Lanham MD: Scarecrow Press, 2000.

Periodicals

Ronald Brownstein — "Chicago Turns Summer into Student Saving Time," *Los Angeles Times*, July 30, 2001.

Milton Chen "Back to School: A Time to Rethink Time," Edutopia, October 19, 2006, www.edutopia.org.

Contra Costa Times "Year-Round Schools Are an Experiment Worth Trying," April 5, 2007.

Don Heinzman "Year-Round School Has Educational Advantages," www.hometownsource .com.

Duke Helfand "Year-Round Discontent at Hollywood High," *Los Angeles Times*, November 20, 2000.

Michael Janofsky "As More Schools Open Earlier, Parents Seek to Reclaim Summer," *New York Times*, August 6, 2005.

Louisville *Courier-Journal* "Teachers See Benefits in Year-Round Schools," July 17, 2006.

Jay Mathews "As Push for Longer Hours Forms, Intriguing Models Arise in D.C.," *Washington Post*, February 5, 2007.

Jean Merl and Erika Hayasaki "L.A. Cuts Back Year-Round Schools," *Los Angeles Times*, September 6, 2005.

Jennifer Mrozowski "Year-Round School Gets Early Start," *Cincinnati Enquirer*, August 6, 2002.

National Education Commission on Time and Learning "Prisoners of Time," April 1994 www.ed.gov/pubs/PrisonersOfTime/ Prisoners.html.

Hilary
Pennington

"Expanding Learning Time in High Schools," *Center for American Progress*, October 2006, www.ameri canprogress.org.

Paul S. Piper

"Year-Round Schools: The Star of the Sea Model," *Pacific Resources for Education and Learning*, www.prel.org.

Mark Pothier

"School's Out: Is It Time We Went to Year-Round Schooling?" *Boston Globe*, August 29, 2004.

Joel Rubin

"More Schools Ditching Multitrack Schedules," *Los Angeles Times*, July 11, 2004.

Teacher Magazine

"Talkback: The End of Summer?" 2007, www.teachermagazine.org.

Charles Whittle

"We Can Pay Teachers More; It's a Matter of Redesigning the Schools," *Washington Post*, September 15, 2005.

Jodi Wilgoren

"Calls for Change in the Scheduling of the School Day," *New York Times*, January 10, 2001.

Index